SUPERGIRL 2 SUPERWOMAN

The Ultimate Guide to Female Leadership

Sheun Oke

Loquats

A catalogue record for this book is available from the British library.

All rights reserved for translation into foreign languages.

Second edition

ISBN 978-0-9933132-1-9 (paperback)

For information on quantity discounts or having this title customized for your organization, please email sheun@sheunoke.com

Printed in Great Britain for SheunOke by The Printing House, 3rd Floor 14 Handover Street, London. W1S 1YH

For Prince Christopher
and
Princess Aderonke Olotu

(Of blessed memories)

TABLE OF CONTENTS

FOREWORD

Leadership is the basis of all we are able to achieve on earth. It takes a vision and appropriate action for anything tangible to be achieved.

In the 21st century, more women are coming forward against odds to blaze the trail. Sheun is one of them.

A female leadership expert, her passion to see the greatness in every single female is palpable. I remember how her eyes lit up when she was discussing this book with me.

Raymond, 'My goal is to provide the ultimate guide to female leadership'. It will be a 'one-stop-shop' for every single woman or girl that aspires to maximize her potential'.

I must say it was a joy coaching her through putting this phenomenal book out to the world.

She has created a marvellous meaning into the word SUPER.

Reading this book, you will discover the mindset for everyday win.

Furthermore you will discover how to speak for influence, package for success, lead yourself and the next generation with integrity. Her focus on self-leadership brings about a total new meaning to peak performance.

I highly recommend you hire her expertise to help you and your organization position for excellence. No matter where you are at your life's journey, she will bring out the SUPER in you.

—Raymond Aaron
New York Times Bestselling Author

FOREWORD

E very now and again, a book comes along that changes the game. This is one such book. A book that gives women the tools to excel in leadership. This book is a must read for every woman and girl seeking success.

I had just returned from New York where I attended the United Nations 59th Session of the 'United Nations Commission on the Status of Women (CWS59)', when Sheun approached me to contribute to this book and to write the Foreword. And as they say, 'There is nothing greater than an idea whose time has come.'

> This incredible book serves to inspire, motivate and change the attitudes of women around the world, spurring them on to go that extra mile to find their talent, to find themselves and their purpose in order to excel in leadership roles, allowing them to compete on equal footing with their male counterparts.
>
> Being the awardee of the prestigious title *'African Woman of the Year'* 2012, and having been honoured as a *Global Official of Dignity; Ambassador for Peace; Humanitarian Ambassador;* and *Africa Goodwill Ambassador, coupled*

with starting and running different successful organizations focused on developing leadership in the female gender, e.g. Justina Mutale Foundation for Leadership and its Global Forum on Women Leadership and Change, I can authoritatively identify with the principles aligned in this book.

It is a masterpiece that is set to change the leadership landscape for women.

If applied correctly, the great leadership tips in this book will enable women to reach their potential and excel as leaders in the 21st century and beyond.

I must commend Sheun on her great timing for writing this book. It has come at a time when the world is just about to embark on the new *Global Goals,* which strongly call for women's empowerment and gender parity in all walks of life. The social dimension of sustainable development puts its emphasis on equity and equality, and this involves confronting negative social trends such as growing income disparities, rising unemployment and a persistent gender gap. This book addresses the challenges and offers some solutions and great tips, for women to rise in leadership roles in order to bridge the gender gap.

Sheun has held leadership positions in several international organizations, whilst also taking time to study gender related issues in conjunction with marketing management and coaching. These magic combinations qualify her to guide women in their leadership journey.

Empowering women and girls to change their role in a culture can play a significant role in society's development and the transformation of culture.

Read this book, apply it and your all round success as a female leader will dramatically improve.

You will learn how to rise from a Supergirl to become a Superwoman!

—Justina Mutale

Co-Author, of *The Journey Behind:*
The Tale of High Profile Professionals

From the Ballroom to the Boardroom,
Founder & President,
Justina Mutale Foundation for Leadership

BOOK REVIEWS

What a perfect time for this masterpiece to be published! Sheun brings to life the total package for every woman to lead with confidence whilst passing the baton to the next generation.

—**Cllr Sade Etti**,
Mayor of Hackney

My fellow, John Maxwell Team Member Sheun, loves to add value. I met her a few years ago at one of our John Maxwell global trainings. I love her passion. She is committed to making sure our amazing teenage girls grow into women who are powerful leaders. Any woman or girl serious about making the most of her life, career, and family must pick up a copy of this book. Men, get a copy for the ladies in your life!

—**Sheri Riley**,
Empowerment Speaker, Life Strategist

Sheun is an embodiment of a self-leader. She is self-motivated and so well qualified to train a new generation of self-leaders. This book surely is a bestseller and I would recommend it to every single female on earth to pick up and read. Looking for a coach to train your team and make them a SUPER success? Then you have your woman.

—**Usen Udoh**,
Group Chief human resources director
Dangote Industries Ltd.

In this book, Sheun revealed the blueprint to breed the next generation of female leaders starting from the cradle.Focusing on solutions rather than the problems, every woman that reads this will ultimately earn the 'SUPER' status!

—Karen White,
Lieutenant Colonel (Retired), United States Air Force
Founder, Dream Finders Coaching, LLC.

She just exudes a joyful-nothing-can-stop-me attitude that I find infectious. Her posts, her photos, her videos and her singing all draw you in. She's confident and bubbly and you just want some of whatever it is she's living on! Reading this book, you will find out what her secrets to 'being Sheun' are. SUPER woman indeed! You want to be the Ultimate SUPERwoman or girl? Rush to get this book, read and digest it.

—Salt Essien,
Author of *The Diary of a Desperate Naija Woman*
series and *True Confessions*

Sheun Oke is a vibrant and upbeat go-getter and you can feel the pulse through this book.She never stops amazing me with her tremendous enthusiasm, energy and persistence. She combines an athletic lifestyle, drive, love for doing good with high leadership octane, making her a coach of choice. This book gives a deeper meaning to SUPER and you cannot but be equipped as a woman to lead in all areas of life. If you are after serious, positive change in your life, Sheun is the person you need to engage!

—Abdulla A Abandi,
Coach, Speaker and Trainer

Sheun nails it! If you are a woman or girl, or you know any at all, then this book is an absolute must read. I really do see a new generation of female leaders emerging and I can see the difference this book is going to make in my girls' lives. As a proud father of two awesome daughters Michelle & Sophia, and a husband to my beautiful wife; there is no doubt that this book will enhance their leadership traits as well as the reader pursuing leadership growth. The content is bigger than the book it was written in and has the potency to catapult you from any level you are now to a position of confident leadership. I highly recommend this to every organization, professionals, entrepreneurs, schools, parents and teachers.

—Nelson Carcamo,
CEO/Founder of NC Consulting Enterprises, Inc.
Executive Coach, Speaker, Teacher,
Trainer, Mentor, & Leadership Development, and
Program Coordinator with The John Maxwell Team

In a world where girls are still striving to be noticed and counted in boardrooms, it is paramount to have tools to prepare for the scramble ahead. Supergirl 2 Superwoman has been written to help mould girls into great leaders, entrepreneurs and innovators. The world needs a change and only leadership can achieve it!

—Pauline Long,
CEO BEFTA awards,
Philanthropist and TV presenter

ACKNOWLEDGEMENTS

To write a book like this takes a lot of support and encouragement and I want to thank all the amazing people who surround my life.

I would not be who I am today and therefore this book would not have been written without the love, support and influence of many people.

To my handsome husband, Stephen, you are my alterego, my rock and the wind beneath my wings. I will treasure you forever.

To my children Rotimi, Bukunmi and Nicole (The Supergirl), all so unique and awesome, I am so proud of the opportunity to be your mum.

Seeing you everyday reminds me of the blessings of God and thanks for understanding even when mum had to focus on writing during your holidays.

To my dad and mum, although you are both no longer with us in flesh, you sowed the seed of greatness in me and have always encouraged me never to settle for less, to carry on being a true princess. I miss you both.

To my dad and mum (by marriage), you are true blessings! Thanks for raising and mentoring the best husband in the whole wide world for me. Your love and perceptive advice are priceless.

To my siblings Tolu Awolola and Yinka Olotu, my very first team! It was really a pleasure growing up and leading you both.

To all the Olotu clan and all the origin of Ikun Akoko, Ondo state, Nigeria, I must say I am proud to be a daughter.

To my mentor John C Maxwell, who inspired me from my teen years to be the best leader I could be, without you this book would never have been written.

To Gerry Roberts, who taught me how to publish a book and grow rich, without your seminar, this book might have ended up a dream for a longer time.

To Raymond Aaron and the entire 10-10-10 book writing program team, you truly inspired me to transform my thinking and to give my clients exchange in abundance.

Thank you Oladunni Owo and Yetunde Adeshile, you came into my life to make my dream a reality. We indeed are 3 musketeers changing the world together.

A big thank you to the amazing SUPERwomen Justina Mutale, Sheri Riley, Irene Olumese, Audrey Joe-Ebigbo, Bidemi Mark-Mordi, Salt Essien-Nelson, Pauline Long, Karen White, Baroness J, Renee Wilbur, Yinka Rose Adepoju, Paula Pritchard, Dr. Michelle Vaughn and a host of others for sharing valuable personal insights and experiences with me.

Thank you to my book architects Vishal Morjaria, CV Pillay and Naval Kumar for all your contributions.

To all the amazing female mentors I have had, Mrs Akinboro, Mrs Sonubi, Mrs Oladipo (my Saint Anne's School principal),

Aunty Fadekemi, Dame Oluremi Oyo (lt), Mrs Odumosu, Chizoma Okoli, Lora Longemeier, Karen Brady, I must say a massive thank you for being who you are.

To my pastors Ken and Christine Williamson, thank you for your uplifting words.

For all that blaze the trail for me to follow in self-development, mindset and speaking: Stephen Covey, Zig Ziglar, Brian Tracy, Bob Procter, Robert Kiyosaki, Mark Victor Hansen, Les Brown and Eric Worre.

To Paul Martinelli- the president of the JMT, all my mentors, faculty members and the awesome leaders on the John Maxwell Team, I duff my hat. You are simply incredible!

To all the Loquats consulting and publishing team, you are the best!

To my marketing team and a world of leaders that surround me, I can only say, what an honour!

It is impossible to conclude this section without mentioning these great men: Mr. Ogunlowore—my English teacher; Usen Udoh—you showed me the possibilities of a young person having a dream; Tony Moka—for giving me my first break in business development; Boye Abe—for your energy and mentoring; and Roddy Galbraith—for teaching me how to speak more.

I could cover the pages of this book with acknowledgements, and it would still not contain all.

I appreciate every single person I have come into contact with in my life's journey so far who has positively impacted me.

Chapter 1

THE JOURNEY BEGINS . . .

Seating in the hall with over 100 awesome authors-to-be, listening to Gerry Robert telling me 'It's time to stop thinking about the book you want to write, start it now!' my thoughts went to the book I have thought about for years. Right there and then, I wrote this title down *Super Girl 2 Super Woman*. But why this book?

I have heard for many years that life has no manual. You just happen by and learn along the way. The routine has been 'grow a little, start school, learn, grow more, learn more, graduate, get a good job, settle down, have a family'. So for several centuries, we just 'happen-by'. Parents follow what they learn from their own parents and just pass it down the generations. Of course, often, vital information is lost. Some children succeed, some don't. Then the cycle repeats itself each time.

There is a joke about a bride cutting off the ends of a turkey on a continuous basis. One day her husband asked her, 'Why do you always cut off those?' She looked at him and thought for a few seconds...'That's the way my mum does it.' Then she picked up the phone and called her mum to ask, 'Mum, why do you always cut off the head and tail of the turkey?' Mum wondered why she asked because they have always done this!

The woman reported back to her husband that is simply the way my mum does it! 'You know what?' he suggested, 'We might as well ask your grand mum at the next reunion.' The next reunion came, and they asked grand mum. 'Grandma, Why do you always cut off the ends of the turkey?' In response, grandma said, 'The ovens during our younger days were much smaller, so we cut off the ends to help the turkey fit in properly.' Really? That's it?

Could this be the case with you today? Are you a reflection of your parents and their worth because you keep repeating what they did in past times? Is there a way I can help you to reflect and challenge the status quo so you actually get what you want, deserve or desire out of your business, career and life?

There is a growing need for female leaders in all spheres of life and new legislation being put into place to encourage this; it's time for you to take your position.

More than 7 billion people on earth? Of course, your expertise is highly needed!

I have discovered that the thirst and search for knowledge has increased in our information age. What if life really does have a manual? What if we can study the lives of those that have lived it, gotten the results we desire and duplicate their path to success? Will we get the same results?

Have you ever wanted more out of life? Have you ever felt you are going through the motions of life and not finding the true fulfilment you desire? Have you ever aspired to be a voice in your space but can hardly hear yourself? What about having that dream? When will it come to pass?

Or you are already successful but considering how to impact more lives and leave a lasting legacy?

'Leadership is influence,' Dr. John C. Maxwell says, and the world is in need of leaders in every field and sphere. In addition, there is a need for more women to add their feminine touch to leadership. Most corporations are now charged with the task of balancing the female to male ratio of board members and increasing women in elective capacities.

I believe in the proverb that says, 'The hand that rocks the cradle rules the world.'

What if you can be mentored and in turn you mentor your girl into becoming a confident leader?

Most of what we do today as adults is the result of unconscious acts. What if these unconscious acts could be broken down and systematized so they could be easily learnt and taught to younger girls?

I remember vividly as a 5 year old that I always loved to be in charge. Yes, I was born that way! Being a first born child gave me my very first shot at leadership. Watching my own daughter Nicole now, I can't but see a mini me—she is opinionated and an outstanding negotiator, communicator, charmer, and motivator, as well as passionate, caring, dreamy, laser-focused, resilient, hopeful and ready to learn. These are some of the main ingredients needed to excel in business, other professional careers and life. That is, if all these qualities are well blended and consciously developed and mastered.

Growing up in the ancient city of Ibadan, Oyo state—the largest and most populous city in Nigeria—was a joy for me. There was so much to see and learn especially the communality and the entrenched moral values.

My father, Prince Christopher Olusuyi Olotu, was an accountant, and my mother, Rev. Aderonke Olotu, was an entrepreneur. Now, both my parents are blessed memories. While alive, they were contrasting figures.

Dad focused on stability while mum was the go-getter. She tested the waters, dropped her great-paying job as a 21 year old and chose a life of entrepreneurship.

I grew up comparing both of my parents, and I must say, consciously or unconsciously, I acquired a lot of wisdom by growing up in this environment.

Self-leadership is the first basis of excelling, and I will show you how you can transform your life by sheer determination to be the very best you can be.

I could go on and on about having a first degree in agricultural economics and an MBA in marketing management, or about being a PRINCE2 certified project manager/risk manager, or about being part of the Institute of Leadership and Management (ILM) in the United Kingdom, or about being a certified member of The John Maxwell Team of speakers, coaches and trainers, but before all these accomplishments comes the passion I have for people and leadership.

My ultimate goal is to infect you with so much passion for purpose as a woman or girl that you go out to positively infect others. After all, passion is contagious.

The world is waiting for you, and I will be with you all the way as a companion to walk you through some of the roadblocks and negative mindsets that could stop you from being all you can be.

The journey evolves as you flip to the next page of this book…

Chapter 2

THE LEADERSHIP WORD BUZZ

The challenge of leadership is to be strong, but not rude; be kind, but not weak; be bold, but not bully; be thoughtful, but not lazy; be humble, but not timid; be proud, but not arrogant; have humour, but without folly.

—Jim Rohn

The word 'leadership' has been a familiar word since I was of a tender age. Being a first child, I was well aware of the responsibility I had towards my two siblings. I heard my dad say several times, 'Don't you know your younger ones are looking up to you for leadership?'

So, without anyone having to describe or define the word to me, I knew leadership meant 'doing the things you want duplicated around you, so you can get a desired result.'

Writing this now makes me smile. As parents, we never know the gravity of lessons our children learn from us at a very tender age.

Now, having grown and having led several teams successfully

over the years, I cannot but define leadership in a more all-encompassing way.

As defined by John C Maxwell 'Leadership is the facilitation of the process of the crystallisation of potential into desired results (cultivated vision) through the systematic organization of talents.'

Keywords and Definitions

Facilitate: To make easier or less difficult; Careful planning *facilitates* any kind of work.

Process: A series of actions or steps taken in order to achieve a particular task.

Potential: Having or showing the capacity to develop into something in the future.

Desired result: Strongly wish for or want an outcome

Systematic: Having a clear and fixed action plan in carrying out a process.

For there to be appropriate leadership, there has to be a vision.

Vision sees the nearest future as if it has happened already. It gives you a clear indication of what arriving at the destination looks like. It is very visual.

The world is looking to see more women in leadership and in several male-dominated fields, so one of your major visions should be to align yourself and your wards to fill these gaps. Your preparation must start now.

Every single person should have a vision for his or her life. After all, if we are embarking on a journey, it only makes perfect sense to sit down to plan our itinerary and costing. (In a later chapter, I will guide you through the process of developing your vision and personal statements).

Dec 2013: I was looking at my profile, 'Oluwaseun olotu-Oke,' on Facebook when suddenly a post from John C. Maxwell popped up that said, 'Join the John Maxwell team today.'

I was intrigued. I had been a student of his for over 15 years and his books have had a positive impact on my life both as a student during university and during my successful career in the financial sector. I also had a 15-year-old dream of meeting him and being a part of the impact he is making around the world.

I decided there and then to join the team. Upon seeking more information, I delved in. The vision was clear. I will be leading nations and helping other women, entrepreneurs, employee-preneurs, mums, students, ministers and politicians to become great leaders by sharing my journey through my books, seminars, trainings, coaching and mentoring. Who better to mentor me in this process than the number one leadership guru in the world?

So it is a pleasure to know you are reading this book now. Even if we have not met yet, I know a part of my vision is being fulfilled. Yes, I saw you before today! How amazing is that!

I took action by joining the JMT University and flying to Orlando, Florida to meet with my mentor, his team and to get officially certified as a coach, speaker and teacher.

Each of the steps required adequate planning and lots of faith but what really gave birth to the planning was the vision of being a great leader. Below, I quote from my favourite book:

> *Write down the vision, make it plain upon the tablets, that he may run that reads it.*
>
> —*Habbakuk. 2 v 2*

There are three key questions a leader must be able to answer affirmatively in order to be successful:

The sensitivity question: Do you care about the people you want to lead?

The ability question: Can you help the people you want to lead?

The trust question: Can you be trusted?

Sensitivity, ability and trust—these are three key qualities of a leader. I refer to them as the leadership SAT.

But how do we put these qualities into perspective?

Leadership is getting pre-determined things done through tapping into the emotional economy of other people.

Justina Mutale, African Woman of the Year in 2012, corroborated this by sharing her belief that leadership is about putting humanity at the centre and acknowledging that a leader works with humans with emotions rather than machines or statistics. 'A leader has to win the hearts and minds of the team and their commitment to go the extra mile,' she emphasizes.

People make leadership work! When you love people, leading them becomes the easiest thing on earth.

Chapter 3

THE WORLD'S BIGGEST CHALLENGE
TO BE SOLVED BY YOU?

*The brick walls are there for a reason. The brick walls are
not there to keep us out. The brick walls are there to give us
a chance to show how badly we want something. Because
the brick walls are there to stop the people who don't want
it badly enough. They're there to stop the other people.*
—*Randy Pausch*

Although the tide is changing and more women are being elevated into leadership roles, there is much work to be done. Glenn Llopis reporting for *Forbes* reports, 'As of July 2013, there were only 19 elected female presidents and prime ministers in power around the globe. Whilst in the business world, women currently hold only 4.6% of fortune 500 CEO positions and the same percentage of Fortune 1000 CEO positions.'

Even with women progressively moving upwards in the business world, we are yet to be fully appreciated for the unique qualities and abilities we bring to the workplace.

Several challenges stand in the way of improving the odds for women.

Major Challenges Faced by Women in Leadership

1. **Stereotyping:** Women feel they need to act like men. Stereotyping is a major challenge facing females. There are some professions that are synonymous with men. Here are 10 major male dominated professions: football, accounting & finance, comedy, computer technology, law enforcement, emergency services, sports media, politics, construction, and motivational speaking.

   Loquats consulting is attempting to bridge the gap. It will be supporting the Waliaprin (walklikeaprincess. org) organization by facilitating girls' and women's entry into these industries by way of capacity building and will be the largest recruitment agency providing confident and leadership ready female workforce.

2. **Tradition:** It has been generally entrenched in tradition that girls or women are mainly for reproductive and domestic purposes. In some countries, girls get married off at a young age, many with their genitals mutilated to suppress their sexuality. This is a major challenge that requires lots of education on the global frontier.

3. **Emotions:** It is so easy to see the emotional strain on a woman if things are not going well around or within them. This is because of the sensitive nature of the female gender. It can create an obstacle to productive work, if not managed appropriately.

4. **Lack of support from other females:** I remember my second stint at managing a regional branch

network of an international bank. I had more support from my male staff than from my female staff. The lack of support network tends to harden the core of female leaders, since it tends to form a defensive mechanism.

5. **Balancing family and career**: Women are still the main caregivers to children as well as the elderly. Consequently, many women can only pursue careers on a part-time basis (especially when their children are young), resulting in fewer promotional opportunities than their male counterparts. One of my mentors and the Vice- Chairperson of Westham Football Club, Karen Brady, describes this challenge in her book, *The strong Woman*: 'I had to go to work after three days' maternity leave and felt miserable all through. It was a mixed feeling of being scared and not wanting to let anyone down, of feeling guilty for having a baby in the first place and not wanting enormous change in my personal life to get in the way of the job I had to do. Most importantly, I was determined my employers wouldn't think I was incapable of carrying on as normal now that I had a baby.'

6. **Policies**: Several policies are put in place to engender gender equality but implementation has been challenging due largely to entrenched traditional beliefs.

Some agencies have been at the forefront of formulating these policies.

Soon after the passage of the 1973 Percy Amendment to the Foreign Assistance Act, USAID established the Women in Development (WID) Office to assist USAID missions and regional bureaus in integrating women into their various development projects.

In 1982, the 'Women in Development' Policy Paper was issued. It was supplemented in 1996 by a Gender Plan of Action (GPA) that included requirements for gender integration in policy, personnel, procurement, performance monitoring, and evaluation. An evaluation of the Plan in 2000 by the Advisory Committee on Voluntary Foreign Assistance (ACVFA) found a number of obstacles to effective institutionalization of the GPA, including large budget cuts coupled with expanding budget earmarks, disruptions caused by reorganization of U.S. foreign assistance agencies, low levels of consultation and communication about the Plan with Agency staff, and concern over proliferation of Agency priorities, among others.

Hilary Clinton said, 'Achieving our objectives for global development will demand accelerated efforts to achieve gender equality and women's empowerment. Otherwise, peace and prosperity will have their own glass ceiling.'

7. **Education and training issues**: Girls have limited access to education in many countries due to some parents' belief that the girls can get by with the basics. Furthermore, women and men learn in different ways. However, most organizations offer the same training to both women and men with only a few developing the right materials for the inclusion of women. One of the schools I admire is Brentwood School. Although a mixed school, girls and boys are taught separately at the junior schools to cater directly to their differing needs. My team and I work with organizations to design a clear path that will ultimately result in breeding more confident girl and women leaders.

8. **Lack of mentorship**: The value of mentorship cannot be over-emphasized. A female that has attained a level of success should look out for the next generation. However, the mentorship culture is more visible in men than women, especially due to the time constraints experienced by women (the work, life and family balance).

Personally, I am a product of mentorship. One of my mentors in the financial sector was Chidinma Okoli, a strong and opinionated leader. I watched her closely and started reaching out to be mentored by her. Easy? Absolutely not!

It takes determination to get access to good mentorship.

My friend Sheri Riley, the founder of Glue Inc and Exponential Living, wanted to get into the entertainment world and searched in earnest for a mentor. In an interview, she said, 'I studied and spent four and a half years researching the entertainment industry, sent out 20 letters each week to top CEOs in the entertainment world (each hand typed—it was way before the advent of the computers) requesting only 15 minutes of mentorship. No one was willing to talk to me. All I got were two CEOs that spent 10 minutes telling me why I could not make it in the entertainment world!'

She eventually achieved her heart's desire and was the first to give the music sensation Usher Raymond IV his first big break when no one believed in him. She went on to work with other music sensations. She has now given her life to providing mentorship for many young people who have gone on to be CEOs and top executives.

Female mentorship should be ingrained in the developmental plan of any organization that is forward-looking in the 21st century and beyond.

In this chapter, we have identified some challenges facing women leaders but the most important thing is to get you ready to solve the world's problem, because without *you* the world is meaningless.

As reported by the Guadian.com, Michele Obama in her 2015 visit to London promoting her 'Let Girls Learn initiative' was at a Muslim school and gave an inspiring speech. In this speech Michele Obama said:

> 'Maybe you feel no one is paying attention to you, you wonder whether it's worth it, to even aspire to be something great,' she told her young audience. 'Maybe you read the news and hear what folks are saying about your religion, and you wonder if anyone ever sees beyond your headscarf to see who you really are, instead of being blinded by the fears and misperceptions in their own minds. And I know how painful and how frustrating all of that can be. I know how angry and exhausted it can make you feel. But here's the thing—with an education from this amazing school, you all have everything, everything, you need to rise above all of the noise and fulfil every last one of your dreams.'

The message is clear—you are not a problem but a solution!

Do you know that you are an exquisite being? Yes indeed. At creation there was extra care taken in forming you and I.

How would I describe you? SUPER!

In the next chapter, I will be sharing the SUPER system with you. It will definitely get you moving into that existing leadership position that already has your name boldly written on it!

Remember, leadership for you as a woman is yours for the asking and taking.

As Bidemi Mark-Mordi, author and CEO of Vertbatim Communications Limited, said in a recent interview, 'No one can keep women out of the boardroom or leadership positions. Every employer is looking for value. You have to bring some value to the table. So think not just in the elegant looks but also in the intellectual/economical contributions.'

Activity

1. Write 5 additional challenges that you think affect female in leadership.

2. Do you have a mentor? Write their name down. What informed your choice of mentor?

3. How can you help your daughter or a female mentee overcome the challenges described in this chapter?

Chapter 4

THE SUPER YOU

The words, 'SUPERgirl 2 SUPERwoman' rang in my ears as I wrote down the title of the first book solely authored by me. I have co-authored, with six other amazing women (Sophie Van Rooyen, Charity Moyo, Fiona Yorke, Roz Bazile, Tamni Durden and compilation done by Anita Bradshaw) a book titled, Reposition for Change (Authorhouse, 2015). In this book, the chapter 'Small girl, big dreams,' addresses the need for everyone to have dreams as early as possible. It is the duty of a parent to help fuel these dreams. It also emphasizes the need to tap into all the social skills learnt as we grow up. To cite from the book:

The value of a genuine smile is worth more than its weight in diamonds.

—Sheun Olotu-Oke

I f you want to reposition for global visibility, then I would encourage you to order a copy at www.sheunoke.com.

Here is one of my favourite anecdotes, which may describe you...

A little boy asked his mum why she was crying. 'Because I am a woman,' she answered.

'I don't understand, '' He said. His mum hugged him and said, 'And you never will.'

Later the boy asked his dad, 'Why does mum seem to cry for no reason?'

'All women cry for no reason,' was all his dad could say.

The little boy grew up and became a man, still wondering why women cry.

Finally, he gave God a call. When God got on the phone, he asked, 'God, why do women cry so easily?'

God answered:

When I made woman, she had to be SPECIAL.

I made her shoulder strong enough to carry the weight of the world yet delicate enough to give comfort.

I gave her inner strength to endure childbirth and rejection that many at times come from her children

I gave her a hardness that keeps her going even when everyone gives up and she takes care of her family through sickness and fatigue without complaining.

I gave her sensitivity to love her children under any circumstances even if they have hurt her badly.

I gave her strength to carry her husband through his faults and fashioned her from his ribs to protect his heart.

I gave her wisdom to know that a good husband never hurts his wife but at times tests her strength and resolve to stand by him in all situations.

And finally, I gave her tears to shed. This is hers exclusively to use whenever it is needed.

You see, my son, the beauty of a woman is not in the lovely dresses, expensive perfumes or jewellery she wears. The beauty of a woman must be seen through her eyes because this is the doorway to her HEART, THE PLACE WHERE LOVE RESIDES.

Wow! Doesn't that just sum it all up? The SUPERwoman that mentors a SUPER generation!

We will be looking at the very meaning of SUPER, which is the acronym I have devised to show you the value of female leadership which is in high demand especially in the 21st century and beyond.

I will be positioning you to lead with integrity and will show you the different examples of women that have done this and made or are still making history. Here it goes...

The SUPER you!

S-Sensitive

U-Undeterred

P-Proactive

E- Elegant

R-Replicator

For the rest of the chapter, I outline each of these qualities in detail.

Sensitive: The Art of Leading with a Heart

Girls display quicker and delicate appreciation of others' feelings more than the male gender largely due to their genetic and behavioural composition.

It is easier to see a girl that wants to feed dolls and push a dummy buggy than to see a boy doing same. There is an innate sensitivity put into the female gender by the creator, which affects the way we handle situations. Girls are more prone to internalizing emotions whilst boys are more external.

This sensitivity almost gets numbed, however, when women enter the corporate or business worlds, mainly because we are trying to be like the 'men' to stay in what has almost been deemed the 'men's world.' But can I reveal a secret to you?

Your sensitivity makes you a better leader!

Mother Teresa, a nun, was a massively influential leader. Although slightly built in frame, she exuded the essence of sensitivity in leadership, spurring other people on to follow in her wake. Here is an excerpt from one of her speeches:

> *I want you to find the poor here, right in your own home first. And begin love there. Be that good news to your own people. And find out about your next-door neighbour - do you know who they are? I had the most extraordinary experience with a Hindu family who had eight children. A gentleman came to our house and said: Mother Teresa, there is a family with eight children, they had not eaten for so long - do something. So I took some rice and I went there immediately. And I saw the children - their eyes shining with hunger - I don't know if you have ever seen hunger. But I have seen it very often. The mother took the rice, divided it up, and she went out. When she came back I asked her - where did you go, what did you do? And she gave me a very simple answer: My neighbours are hungry also. What struck me most was that she knew who they were and they were a Muslim family. I didn't bring more rice that evening because I wanted them to enjoy the joy of sharing. But there were those children, radiating joy, sharing the joy with their mother because she had the love to give. And you see this is where love begins - at home. We think sometimes that*

poverty is only being hungry, naked and homeless. The poverty of being unwanted, unloved and uncared for is the greatest poverty. We must start in our own homes to remedy this kind of poverty.

Sensitivity is one of the questions your followers want answered in the affirmative. It is a power that a female leader wields, and it multiplies your influence beyond measure.

Does she care about me? This is a sensitivity question. Now, it is time to sharpen your sensitivity and assume your position as the next effective leader.

Ways to Compound Your Sensitivity

1. Know your own strengths and weaknesses as a leader. I would recommend a great book that helped me in this regard, *The Strength Finder by Tom Rath.*

2. Seek to improve on your weaknesses by taking on constructive criticism.

3. Be a good listener. Your team should be comfortable to share their struggles and triumphs with you. This helps you connect with them at a level that cannot be under-estimated.

4. Be great at offering public praise. Everyone loves to be appreciated. Make it a point of duty to praise more than give rebuke.

5. Train your team to duplicate your areas of strength and surround yourself with people that compliment your weakness

Undeterred: The Power of Desire and Determination

In life, we suffer several setbacks and even defeats. Persevering despite these setbacks is the definition of being undeterred. Determination is fuelled by intense desire. Knowing exactly what you want and refusing to settle for less will get you to your destination even in the face of adversity.

You cannot have what you do not strongly desire.

Let's take a typical example from the very first ever female prime minister—Sirimavo Bandaranaike. Born into a prominent family as the eldest of six children, she married Sir Solomon Dias Bandaraike who was a prime minister, but his term was cut short in his 3rd year, when he was assassinated by a Buddhist monk.

The widow was distraught, but she decided to step up her game and was put forward as the legitimate successor to her husband's party leadership. She had always had her eyes on leadership. On the 21st of July 1960, Sirimavo Bandaranaike was elected prime minister of Sri Lanka, thus becoming the first ever female prime minister in the world!

What was her major strength? She could not be deterred. She used her setback to her advantage and was popularly referred to as the 'weeping widow.'

She made a capital of her husband's death, going around the villages, showing care and weeping over the children. Yes, she had her other flaws but she made history rather than succumb to her setbacks.

Her daughter, Chandrika Kumaratunga, would go on to become the 4th Sri Lankan executive president, whilst her son, Anura Bandaranaike, would serve as speaker and cabinet member.

If there's one person who knows how to turn impossible challenges into unlimited possibilities it's Renee Wilbur. I met her recently through the John C. Maxwell leadership training group. I was intrigued by the buzz Renee is creating on social media sites regarding a phenomenal platform for entrepreneurs and business owners, so I contacted her to hear her story.

As a top sales leader, small business owner and corporate executive, Renee's talents are evident in everything she does.

Since her childhood, she knew what it was like to be in desperate need of support and resources. It occurred to her that there wasn't a faster, more efficient way for others to get the support and resources they need – when they needed them. So over a four-year time frame, she developed a way.

Renee's passion led her to become an award-winning entrepreneur by finding a way to localize the Internet in ways that no one has ever dreamed of. Her drive and ingenuity, combined with innate resourcefulness, became the foundation for creating something that filled an untapped need on the Internet. The result is ReciProty.

ReciProty is a ground-breaking resource exchange and trusted networking hub that that combines the best of business networking, marketing, community support, and social media linking into one robust platform.

Renee did not stop there. She is now the President of Wilbur Resources International (WRI), the Global Director for Network with Results International (NWRI) and a John Maxwell certified team member. With all of her networking expertise and business knowledge, Renee can help business owners and their corporate sales teams quickly turbo charge the sales process at every level, thereby putting profits into the hands of entrepreneurs and business owners almost immediately. She is absolutely undeterred.

Heard about the most powerful woman in the world, Angela Merkel? A dogged woman indeed! Angela Merkel is a German politician best known as the first female Chancellor of Germany and one of the architects of the European Union.

Her name was Angela Dorothea Kasner at birth, which was in Hamburg, Germany, July 17, 1954. The daughter of a Lutheran pastor and teacher who moved his family to the east to continue his theological studies. She studied physics at Leipzig University, earning a doctorate in 1978, and later worked as a chemist at the Central Institute of Physical Chemistry of the Academy of Sciences between 1978 to 1990.

She entered the world of politics after the 1989 fall of the Berlin Wall, rose to the position of Chairperson of the Christian Democratic Union party, and finally became the first Chancellor of Germany and one of the leaders of the European Union after the 2005 national elections.

During the 2005 elections, Merkel narrowly defeated German Chancellor Gerhard Schröder, winning by just three seats, and after the CDU approved a coalition agreement with the Social Democrats (SPD), she was declared the first female Chancellor in Germany.

She was the very first woman to lead Germany and still got re-elected for a second term in 2009. Merkel did not just wish to be a leader; she also took decisive steps to achieve it. She was not afraid to be criticized.

Merkel had been best in her class during high school. At university in the 1970s, she delved into physics because she relished the challenge of 'something that didn't come easy.' It was also the only subject she ever failed in school—a field that produces results by scientific method and experimentation, rather than gut instinct.

Growing up this way made Merkel a fighter. 'Everything was always a struggle: to avoid attracting attention at all costs, to always be a little bit better than the others,' she said.

Of course, becoming anything note-worthy in life requires dogged determination. The proof is in the pudding. Give your daughter a head-start by teaching these values. If you want it, you have got to go after it unflinchingly.

Note: *Superwomen raise super children!*

You are not just raising girls, you are also raising worthy sons to take care of the women folks.

My friend Audrey Joe-Ezigbo, the CEO of Falcon Corporations observes, 'Everyone is looking to empower the girls and that is great. What about training the boys that would be confident enough to handle these 'powerful female leaders that are being trained?'

I am sure we will be covering that topic in the near future. A dad is a girl's first male role-model. My dad sure was and my husband is for our SUPERgirl.

How Can You be Undeterred?

1. **The Fuel of Determination is Strong Desire:** The fuel of determination is a burning desire to be and to do—it is the starting point from which any major achievements stems.

    My very first job was with one of the largest banks in Nigeria, Zenith bank. I started off as a cashier but later moved to business development. I enjoyed building rapport with clientele, and it was so easy for customers to connect with me. For this reason, my record of new accounts opened swelled over time. Moving to business development/sales and marketing was a smooth transition.

    However, I was passed up on promotions twice,

though I had worked extra hard and had obtained excellent appraisals from my line managers. I would say both were largely due to going on maternity at the wrong time.

I had a strong desire to advance my career rapidly but this would inadvertently stifle the process. So, I worked harder, became even more cheerful, kept on justifying my case to the management until finally, I got it!

The following year saw me getting promoted almost four times and moving on to higher responsibilities within other organizations, just like I had mapped out. This more than compensated for the lost time.

A strong desire will fuel your ambition and will keep the fire of your determination burning.

2. **Clear Goal Setting:** This involves the development of an action plan designed to motivate and guide a person or group towards achieving a set goal. A study done by Edwin A Locke and some of his colleagues shows that specific and ambitious goals lead to more performance improvement than easy or general goals. Goals give you the ability today to do create the future you want.

In 1979, interviewers asked a series of questions to new graduates from the Harvard's MBA Program and found that:

> 84% had no specific goals at all
>
> 13% had goals but they were not committed to paper
>
> 3% had clear, written goals and plans to accomplish them

In 1989, the interviewers again interviewed the graduates from same Harvard class, now ten years older. You can guess the results:

> The 13% of the class who had goals were earning, on average, twice as much as the 84 percent who had no goals at all.

> Even more staggering was the fact that the 3% who had clear, written goals were earning, on average, ten times as much as the other 97% combined.

Where do you want to be in one, three or ten years time? It's time to write down your goals and get SMART.

Your goals must be SMART:

S- Specific

M-Measurable

A-Action oriented

R-Realistic

T-Time based

(For more, on how to write SMART goals visit www. sheunoke.com)

3. **Affirmations:** This is a way of connecting emotions to the goals you have written down. See yourself achieving your goals and say it like you mean it.

   Affirmations are self-suggestions and are the agent of communicating between the parts of mind where thoughts take place and that which serves as the seat of action for the subconscious mind.

In a nutshell, convince your subconscious that you *are* what you want to be.

This is a major part of you becoming what you purpose to be.

Examples of affirmation:

I am so happy and grateful now.

Each day is filled with inspirations, joy, hope, new opportunities and actions.

I have met and exceeded all my goals in the year (insert the present year) with commitment, discipline and unwavering devotion.

I have an awesome team!'

One of my favourite quotes from the good book

Death and life are in the power of the tongue and those who love it will eat its fruit. (Proverbs 18 vs 21)

You have the power to create by words. Saying your affirmations daily and even getting specific with your expectations create a sense of achievement which ends up informing your actions.

Actions lead to achievements.

Activity

Take a 10 minute break from reading this book and write down your affirmations now!

4. **Consistent Action:** Above all, take action daily.

Leaders are readers. Get materials that will help you become. Your reading this book tells me you are on the right path. You must have a clear action plan to achieve your goals daily.

Quick question? Have you written your affirmation? If not, take a short break and do that just now. It is an investment of time well worth it.

Pro-active: The Art of Creating Your own Weather

Proactive is a word that got my notice when I was about 8 years old. It was a Saturday afternoon, and I was in the living room where I had been playing with my siblings. We had just finished our snack time, eating the shortcake made by the popular Nigerian brand of Okin and Parmalat chocolate drink.

Everywhere, the room was littered with biscuit crumbs and my siblings had discarded their drink case right on the floor. On hindsight, it must have looked pretty bad to someone just walking in.

My dad walked in, towering over us, wearing his brown French suit (he was over six feet tall). 'Sheun, can you see how messed up this whole place looks? Do you really need to wait for anyone to tell you before cleaning this whole mess up! You must learn to be pro-active!' he shouted.

It was a rare occasion that he would ever raise his voice. Now as a parent, I could understand the emotions behind my dad's words.

I guess I understood the word 'pro-active' straight from his statement.

Pro-activeness is an action and result oriented behaviour that spurs you to act instead of waiting for things to happen or being told to make things happen. It is about the ability to foresee a problem and put action plans in place to solve them.

In the *7 Habits of Highly Effective People*, Stephen Covey observes, 'Our behaviour is a function of our decisions and not our condition. We can subordinate feelings to values. We have initiative and the responsibility to make things happen.'

Now, did I catch you wondering? Have you been re-active or pro-active?

Reactive people are often affected by their environment (e.g., no one attended university in my family; therefore, I do not need to attend one).

Yes, as much as it does not take a university degree to be successful in life, it gives you an edge it one must be 'appropriately educated' to be massively successful.

Appropriate education means getting to understand the nitty-gritty of the vocation you plan to pursue.

An example of a woman without a university degree, who nevertheless lectures at Harvard University among others, is Nike Okundaye. She is the face behind the huge success story of Nike Arts Gallery, located in Lagos, Abuja and Osogbo. Born in her native village of Ogidi, Ijumu Local Government Area, Kogi State, young Nike had big dreams of what kind of future she wanted for herself. But her dreams were cut off before they could take shape when she lost her mother at age six.

She was taken to her grandmother (who was then the head of all weavers in the community) to live. She started weaving different materials including Adire, a traditional painted cloth design, stopping formal education.

Before her demise, Nike's mum taught her the value of hard work through her own tireless working. Nike never went to school to study art, a vocation that brought worldwide attention. The art had been passed down from her great-grandmother, the late Mrs. Ibikunle. She had to work her way up the different levels of learning to become an expert.

The product of the famous art movement Osogbo, Nike is now recognized worldwide as an artist and textile designer, bringing a vivid imagination and a wealth of history and tradition to the production of Adire.

Her works are celebrated in the main capitals of the world with works exhibited in countries like the United States, Belgium, Germany, Japan and Italy among others. Now, I call that 'appropriate education.' So do not be deterred if you have not attended a university or any higher school of learning yet, reading this book shows you are in search of 'adequate education.'

Proactive people can carry their own weather with them. Whether it rains or shines, there is no difference.

In fact, I tell my clients, 'you have the capacity to create your own day by the way you start it.'

I encourage my family and clients to start their day the way I start mine. Here goes...

Once I open my eyes and have a big smile and a stretch, I say, 'It's a beautiful day,' I also post it on my Facebook page— Oluwaseun Oke'or Sheun Olotu-Oke. So for a daily dose of that, hook up with me on FB.

Boom! The day has started in full force! Indeed, even while writing this, my husband walked towards me and asked why I was smiling.

Since I started this routine in the year 2014, it has gained some followers, and I have several testimonials of the positive impact this has been having on their days.

Being proactive requires taking initiative and does not necessarily mean you are being pushy, obnoxious or aggressive. It means you recognize your responsibility to make things happen.

I relocated to the United Kingdom in 2010 with my family. I was a high flyer from my country, yet I recognized that there may be some challenges in getting into the system and improving on my earning power.

I proactively went to take a course in professional hairstyling and barbering at the celebrity hairstylist's salon, Bobbies Signature, Ikeja. It was normally a one-year course, but I paid to do an executive intensive course, which lasted for 4 months.

I had to humble myself. Yes, I had a masters degree. Yes, Bobby's signature had been my stylist for years and the proprietor himself was shocked when I told him I was there to learn. He knew my elite social status.

In order not to raise any eyebrow, I always park my Corolla 2008 model at a distance.

Was I being stupid? No! A woman has got to be adaptable and any skill gained will always come in handy.

During the time of endless job applications and heartbreaking 'Unfortunately, you have not gone through this time around' responses, I was able to build a hairstyling clientele base of over 300 people and earned enough to make a full-time employee jealous.

According to my friend Raymond Aaron, *The New York Times* best-selling author, 'You can create your own economy'.

You create your own economy by being proactive.

Elegance: The Power of the Right Image

Creating the right image is the essence of any lady. As a trail blazer, you must dress for where you are headed and not where you are presently. It makes a lot of sense, doesn't it?

When you get invited to an occasion, do you dress for the occasion now or do you wait until you are at location before dressing up?

Now is the time to pep up on your elegance, even if you are not yet at your dream position or job.

I define elegance as the graceful and stylish appearance or the attitude that you must exhibit at all times. There is a popular saying, 'dress the way you want to be addressed.' I discovered this secret at a very early age—of course, with the help of my parents.

A woman or girl must have a 'presence.' This is why most aristocrats are sent to finishing schools to learn the art of 'grace.'

Have you ever dressed well and felt like the whole world is at your feet? Or have you ever dressed so 'out of place' for an occasion you felt like hiding away? As I like to say, 'Dress the way you want to feel. Dress the feel.' I must say, most of the things I know now come from reading far and wide. Especially since I set a personal goal to never be mediocre in life, I have come to take elegance seriously.

Basic Ingredients to Help You Polish Up Your Elegance

1. Dress the way you want to be addressed.

Different occasions warrant different types of dressing. For interviews and corporate meetings:

Business professional: A good pair of skirt-suits or pant suits with a camisole to add some colours. Most corporate organizations favour dark coloured suits (e.g., navy blue, black or gray). However, a lady can get away with red, pink, green and all the other colors, especially in the advertising and marketing industry.

Business casual: Dress codes have relaxed at many organizations and business casual is now the norm in many workplaces every day of the week. The challenge is, many people have no idea what this means.

Limit jeans to Friday and be sure they are well ironed: For the rest of the week, when business casual means not wearing trousers and a blouse or sweater, just remember that you never know when a meeting with a client will come up or when you have to go out for an impromptu function with colleagues.

Accessories (e.g., earrings and necklaces) should be kept minimal: Pearls are great and they don't have to be the expensive since there are some great imitations and with same effect.

Corporate dinners: Dresses are the most appropriate. However, you could get away with a pant suit or jumpsuit if it is appropriate (not too casual).

Black long length evening gown

Everyone knows that you should avoid clothes that are too tight or too skimpy. If your clothing is overly revealing, you may be getting attention for the wrong reasons. But baggy clothing that is two sizes too big can be just as detrimental. When choosing work outfits, stick to items with a contemporary cut and avoid anything that is ill-fitting or too large. Wearing something that fits you well will give you that extra boost of confidence.

2. **The elegant lady and room impression.**

Open the door, step in with a confident smile, eyes on the room occupant, still facing the inside of the room, close the door gently behind you and offer an outstretched hand for a firm handshake.

Remember: A smile is the completing accessory for your outfit. Without it, you are half-dressed.

3. **Maintain a good posture.**

Most ladies (different ages) approach me to ask, 'How do you walk in those heels?'

My response has always been the same (never without a smile though), 'But you can see me walking!'

I started wearing high heels at about 10 year of age (so, yes, I have had decades of practice)!

I still remember the colour of my first pair, which were lemon Green. They had straps around the ankles to help train me and keep the shoe in a graceful position.

Wearing high heels help you walk straighter; it helps your spine from slouching, especially to maintain a balance.

Walking straighter, of course, helps you to feel and also appear more confident.

There are roughly about 30 types of heels, although I favour stilettos and platforms.

Itemized below are just a few options…

Kitten Heels

They are ideal for work or events where you do not need the extra height, but will still spend a while on your feet.

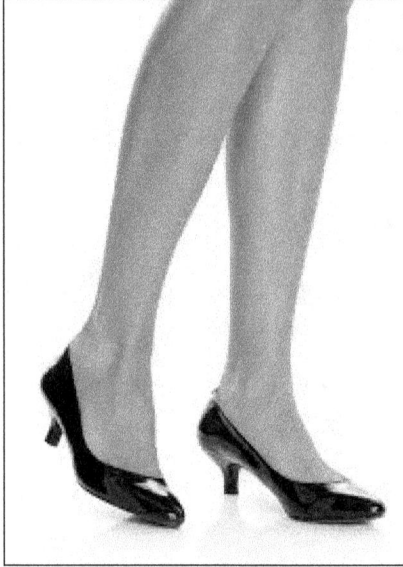

Stilettos

The highest of all the high heels, stilettos can reach up to 9 inches. While these heights can cause problems walking for many, it's a worthy skill for the lengthening effect they have on one's legs. Note: many stilettos are also platforms due to the height (see below for platforms).

I have a favourite 9 inch shoe and trust me, it has its own amazing confidence effect coupled with being a great conversation starter once I notice it got your attention.

Call me vain if you want to, but when you are a networker like me, you will use every tool to connect with your audience. My shoes are generally great conversation starters.

Ankle Strap Heels

The height of the heel can vary, but the one common denominator is the strap that goes around the ankle, making the heels more secure and comfortable to walk in. This was the type I started out with as a 10yr old. Although with block heels.

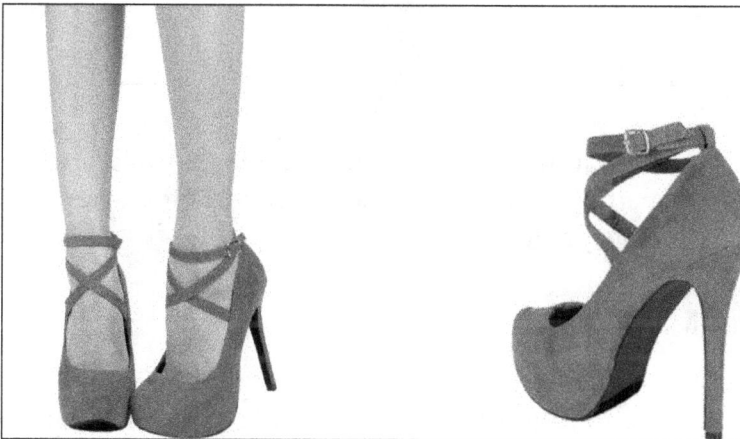

Wedge Heels

There are two different types of wedge shoes: wedge heels and wedge sandals. Wedge heels are flush just like a high heel would be, and there is no separation from the heel to the sole. These are great for you especially is you are on the 'plumper' side: size 14 and above.

A wedge with a strap can give you the lift whilst also supporting your balance. Having the right footwear is absolutely crucial.

4. Makeup Artistry

'Beauty is in the eyes of the beholder' – this is something that we do hear on a regular basis. Using make-up artistry, you can polish up on areas that make you feel less than perfect.

Choosing the right make up for the right occasions is important. A lady must 'have it together' at all times.

There are several ways to learn how to have the right applications these days especially with the advent of YouTube.

My foray with applying makeup began when I was in my 2nd year of university. I had a friend, Evelyn, who knew how to add colour to her face without looking too overly made up. I decided to explore too (I don't mean to sound my own trumpet; I had always looked really beautiful without a make-up and almost boyish in my attitude to extra adornment). Evelyn had all the 'gadgets,' and my role was to sit as the canvass and await the 'great reveal'!

It would have been lovely to have a before and after picture then, but we were not yet blessed with the advanced technology of having a camera on a mobile phone. On concluding her artistry, Evelyn brought a mirror to my face and voila! I loved what I saw! Of course, I had some of my own makeup accessories ready by the time we resumed the next semester.

Makeup Artistry for Every Occasion

For a job interview: Your goal is to enhance your natural features, not overshadow them. Going for an interview wearing heavy makeup could get you off on the wrong footing.

Wear your skin flawless: A very light foundation that matches your colour (I suggest you test before you buy). Ensure your foundation doesn't look too heavy, to avoid ending up with a caked face of making you look chalky. Office lighting can be terrible, so a neutral pink blush or bronzer is the key to looking healthy. You can blend it in quickly with your fingers, perfect for a last-minute touch-up.

Enhance your eyes subtly: Thick black eyeliner and glittery shadows should be left for informal outings. Professionals recommend a plum or soft brown on the lid and into the crease.

Limited gloss: Too much gloss can make you look like you're drooling. Wear a hydrating, long-lasting neutral pink or peach lipstick.

Nails: Avoid wearing glittery nails to the office. I preferably keep my nails well manicured and only use neutral colours (e.g. peach or neutral colour). You want to be remembered for all the right reasons.

You could play around with more colours if you work in a creative industry (e.g., advertising).

You got the offer?

Awesome! The best tip I have for you is to look around, mirror your surrounding and or your boss. Remember, 'people do what people see.' However, there are some organizations that have dress codes; this could point you in the right direction too.

Explore the red lip: Contrary to popular belief, you can actually use the red lipstick to work. Red lips makes you l appear more confident. There are different shades to explore from different brands.

Perfumes: **Perfumes are really great and could help you leave an impression long after you are gone. The rule of thumb is to wear them light. Try scents with ingredients like rosemary. studies suggest that the smell can improve mental performance - or vanilla, which is linked to creativity.**

For a business presentation? If it is to a small group of people, you're in an intimate setting, then play up your eyes. You'll be close enough to your audience to make a connection with them. To make your eyes look bigger, use a peach pencil on your waterline. If you're in a larger space, let your lips be a focal point with a bold, matte, long-lasting shade.

If you feel nervous, try a bronzer instead of a blush. Polls show that women with tans feel more confident. If you are an African like me, your deeper-coloured blush is a great enhancement.

5. The Business Dinner

Explore colours that match well with your outfit. Here is your chance to get all glittery and shimmery. The watchword word, however, is 'moderation' at all times. As a leader, you would need to attend different functions, meetings and presentations. Lots of business dinners and award nights too! You had better been prepared with the right 'Dinner etiquettes' to avoid any form of embarrassment which could make you lose face or at the worst, a great business.

Below are my top tips for business dinners.

1. Be punctual! Arriving at dinner late implies that you are irresponsible and inconsiderate. No one likes a late-coming employer/co-worker so if you are late to dinner, you are automatically starting off on the wrong foot. However, if you do anticipate on being late, give the host a courtesy call beforehand.

2. Do not anticipate where your seat is. It is important to wait to be shown or directed to where to sit.

3. Cell phones should be switched off, left in the purse away from the table. Do not make the mistake of keeping your purse on the table.

4. The basic table setting will include a couple of forks on the left side and knives on the right side. The rule here is to start on the outside. That means the fork farthest away from your plate is for the salad, or appetizer that requires use of fork.

5. Use both fork and knife to cut your food. Remember not to leave the fork halfway on the plate and halfway on the table as some erroneously do.

6. Avoid slurping when eating soup. The sound is embarrassing.

7. Fold your napkin and place on lap. If it drops, do ask for another. Avoid bending over as much as possible. If you must, ask to be 'excused.'

8. Know your glasses. Depending on the formality of the restaurant, there can be up to four glasses at the table, situated in a square pattern. The top left glass is for red wine, below that is for white wine. The top right is for champagne, with the remaining glass for water.

9. Only start eating after all present at the table have been served. If you start with the bread basket, don't forget to pass it to the person on your left.

10. Some subjects are off-limits at the dinner table (e.g., Religion, sex, politics or other controversial topics). Be warned!

11. Just relax and eat! Only take small pieces/bites at a time.

12. Avoid ordering foods that could make a mess.

13. To eat a whole chicken, use your fork and knife. To eat a whole fish, start on one side of the spine and eat from top to bottom. When you're all done, gently lift the bones and discard. Avoid flipping the fish over.

14. If you are on an interview, do not order alcohol, even if there are wine glasses on the table. Just order iced tea or strawberry lemonade. For other business types of dinner, some wine might be ordered. Shadow your host and order a glass of wine as well.

15. Dress conservatively, but properly for the occasion! (We already have this covered earlier).

16. Be very polite and always remember to say the important two letter-words, 'thank you' or 'may I'?

17. Keep your elbows off the table, sit up straight and don't lean back in your chair. I know it seems like a lot to take in, but good practice will get you there.

18. Do not skip coffee and dessert time! This is a time to 'close the deal' and bond with your host.

19. When all is done, remember to thank the host for a great dinner.

A big secret? Avoid ordering crabs, lobsters and shrimps.

Remember the film *Pretty Woman*? Yes, some awkward moments can arise when you realize you need special equipments to eat a lobster!

Being elegant at all times is important for leaders or aspiring leaders. Remember, you are leading a new generation of people, and you want to achieve a lasting legacy!

When is the best time to teach this? As early as a child can understand being corrected. I would suggest from age 4.

Exploring and teaching this now will distinguish you and your mentee, which may also be your child.

Replicator: The law of the picture

Ever heard 'she is just your replica'? Replicating means to make an exact copy of or duplicate.

The beauty of creation is in the ability for like to reproduce like. This is a very important aspect of breeding the next generation of female leaders. You cannot give what you do not have.

Parenting or mentoring the next generation of girls to become confident leaders lies in your hands and not just in the school institutions.

Studies have shown that a girl child is pretty much used to stereotyping. By age 4, she is already taking in their environment and forming opinions of what or who they can be.

My daughter, then 4 years old, made an observation about school: 'Mum, why is it that it is only boys who can play football?' I asked her why she thought so.

She said, 'At break time, it's only boys who are allowed to play football and girls just play catch.'

There and then, I asked her if she loved playing football and the answer was 'Yes.' I showed her some female footballers, and we got her a full football kit.

She was so proud and posed for a picture with her dad behind the lenses.

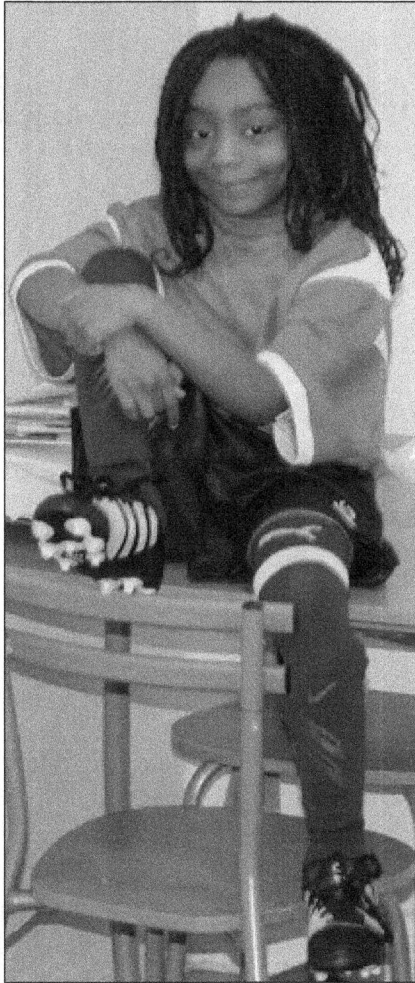

She still has to tussle with her brothers to get the ball at times, but I have planted a seed for her to be able to stand her ground when dealing with them.

One of my earlier mentors as a teen is my aunt-Fadekemi. She is the last of my mum's siblings while I am the first grandchild, so we pretty much are the closest in generation.

She was stylish, bold, brilliant, enterprising and beautiful. I just wanted to be like her so much that I wanted to walk with a limp just like her (the limp was as a result of having medical issues with her right leg). I almost prayed for a limp and my wishes almost got granted because I got to a stage when my right limbs started growing faster than my left!

Replication is synonymous to succession. And you can agree with me that success without successor is tantamount to massive failure.

John Maxwell talked about the 'law of the picture' in his book, *21 Irrefutable Laws of Leadership*.

It simply says, 'People do what people see.'

If your daughter, mentee or team members were to turn out exactly like you, would you love the outcome?

It's a very deep question that you should ponder.

If the answer is no, then it is high time you made a change.

Now, I have not written this, because I don't have my own challenges too. In fact, I have a knack for shoving my clothes into my wardrobe. You know why? I seem to be too much in a hurry to find things in my wardrobe. I just pull everything out and shove them back in with the intent to rearrange them later. All the while my daughter has been watching this bad habit. Once day, her dad went into her room and all her clothes were in total disarray.

'Nicole, why is your wardrobe so messy?' he asked.

'I just love shoving my clothes, just like mum!' she responded.

Of course, you know that spells trouble for me, don't you?

Your team is a direct reflection of you.

If you are humble and grateful, your team will be humble and grateful.

If you are warm and engaging, your team will be warm and engaging.

If you are even-tempered and unflinching under fire, your team will be even-tempered and unflinching under fire.

If you are elegant, your team will be elegant.

If you are a hard worker, your team will be hard working.

Gandhi said, 'Be the change you want to see in the world.' I would add, 'Be the change you want to see in your organization.' Set a new standard. Let your word become flesh. This is the most powerful thing you can do to change your world.

Activity

Evaluate the SUPER you right now. Score yourself on a scale of 1-10 for each (1 being the lowest and 10 highest), add it all together, multiply by 2 and then divide by 10.

SUPER (sensitive, undeterred, proactive, elegant and replicator)

The SUPER Range: 1-4 (mini); 5-7 (midi); 8-10 (ultimate)

Let us evaluate Elizabeth (the leader of a charity organization).

The SUPER Evaluation Table

Attributes	Score	Score x2	SUPER level
Sensitive	6	12	
Undeterred	6	12	
Proactive	7	14	
Elegant	5	10	
Replicator	5	10	
Total	29	58	
Score x2 /10		5.8	Midi

Elizabeth has come out as Midi SUPERwoman. Can you decipher what she needs to do to become the Ultimate SUPERwoman?

Wherever you are right now, our goal is to get you to be the Ultimate SUPERwoman or SUPERgirl.

If you are ready to be at the 'choice' organization (or maybe you already are but need to polish the image of your executives), then you should teach the value of being SUPER in your organization.

We will create a step-by-step program for you to help implement the system.

Chapter 5

HOW TO BE SUPER:
THE SELF-LEADERSHIP MASTERY

Self leadership is a concept that is here to stay. In fact, until I recently put a name to it, it has been the propeller for all the amazing successes I have experienced both in life, career and family. This is a concept I am lending my full energy to teach, train and research more. It will continue to gain more and more popularity as the 21st century evolves and as the whole economy embraces self-mastery.

Brett Steenbarger, a contributor for Forbes.com, writes, 'Now, just think of your life as a diversified organization. You are in the business of living. Your business consists of a career and managing the associated workloads, opportunities, and challenges. Your business also consists of managing a home and its maintenance. The people living within your home? Yes, your business includes managing their needs, from the school and recreational needs of children to the social and emotional needs of spouses. When you think about it, you are the CEO of a rather diversified enterprise.'

If every enterprise requires adequate leadership, how much more you?

Self-leadership is the process of influencing yourself to use all the resources within and around you to establish the self-direction and self-motivation needed for your peak performance.

A leader is a visionary. So if you are leading yourself first, what do you envision?

Aristotle said, 'A soul never thinks without a picture.' We all think in pictures.

I have always had a very vivid mental picture of where and what I wanted to be, however, I only got to create a physical vision board when I got involved in the multi-level marketing industry.

My very first vivid imagination to become a leader outside my home was when I was in the primary school.

I wanted to be the class captain. I attained this in my 6th year, by being the assistant to my male friend-Olawale Aro. But trust me, I know how to take charge.

We reconnected on Facebook after several years and in a catch-up discussion with him, he had this to say:

> Sheun Olotu, you have always had the fire in your eyes. Your drive was palpable even as a young girl. You don't know how to slow down. You want it done and done now. I remember an instance when the teacher asked us to blacken the chalk-board (This was 1987, we didn't have whiteboards and the use of markers then) using a mixture of charcoal, water and some leaves called Ewe Ipin (botanical name: Ficus Exasperata). The boys were still messing around. You just took charge, painted the whole blackboard and ended up with a blackened face and uniform'! You walked off with no cares at all- leaving all the boys staring after you.

In fact, I am not in the least surprised with the tremendous progress I see you have made now. You always were the bold and selfless leader'

In my University, I had a mental picture of changing the order of things. Normally, males are the class representatives whilst females tend to be the assistant. I purposed in my heart to be the very first departmental female representative that would have a male assistant.

Just like I purposed, it happened! I became the first female rep for the Ladoke Akintola University of Technology (LAUTECH), Department of Agricultural Economics, with my able assistant being the gentleman, Valetine.

As a woman thinketh, so she is!

It is never too early to have a vision. In reality, a lot of us got into the corporate world before ever knowing the seriousness of having a vision written down.

You can start fuelling your children's visions by the sort of educational materials or programs you expose them to, even by the time they are a year old.

With John C Maxwell in Orlando, Florida

The Personal Vision Statement

Your vision is your dream. It is the mental picture you carry of yourself, family and community and by which everything you do or become in life are defined.

It must be well articulated and communicated to the appropriate people especially family members.

There are certain elements that a vision statement should possess:

1. It must inspire you to become the person that achieves it.

2. It must cover a wide range and should be diverse enough to include others that will contribute to making it happen.

3. It must be easy to communicate to others.

4. It must include your values (e.g., dedication, loyalty, credibility, honesty, accountability, dignity, respect etc.).

What is a Mission Statement?

Mission statement: A mission statement describes what you want now and how you will achieve your long term aspiration. A mission statement does not define a long term future state but is more concerned with the present state. It answers the questions of: 'What do I do?', 'How do I do it?', 'Who do I do it for?', 'What makes me different', and 'What is the benefit?' It talks about the present leading to the future, and how you will get to where you want to be.

Example: My mission is to help develop Super-female leaders across the world, starting from the cradle, by educating, motivating, inspiring and creating an atmosphere for continuous growth and networking

The 2nd Habit in Stephen Coveys famous book *7 habits of Highly Effective People* says, 'Begin with the end in mind.'

In order to get the most value from this exercise, I suggest you combine the two into a vision and mission statement. Define the overall essence of what you want to achieve and then look at what you are doing to achieve it.

Because we are different, personal mission statements vary but there are some common elements.

What Makes a Good Vision and Mission Statement?

A good vision and mission statement is concise and inspirational.

It's easy to memorize and to repeat.

It should be clear, engaging, realistic, and describe a bright future.

It should furthermore state your intentions, summarize your values, and demonstrate your commitment to living up to these values.

Ideally, the vision and mission statement should also be aligned with the values, culture and possibilities of the organization you currently work for. If your personal values and aspirations are being matched by your employer's, or the industry you want to thrive in, it will be much easier to progress and fulfil your dreams.

However, if your goals are far beyond what the firm can offer, you will need to be honest and assess if the job is still a good match for you.

With a strong vision and mission statement, it's easier for you to evaluate in which industry and company you should invest your time and energy.

How do you go about writing it? What are the steps?

When composing your own statement, find a quiet place where you feel at ease and where you will not be interrupted. Then follow the steps and guiding questions below.

Step 1: Answer the following questions as honestly as you can.

What personal qualities do you most want to emphasize in yourself?

How can you use and display these qualities in a working environment? What are the most important values you want to express at work?

Step 2: Visualize yourself five years from now.

Imagine that you are living the life of your dreams. Envision that everything is exactly the way you want it to be: the type of job or business you are running, the industry it is in, its size and complexity, the people involved, and your own capabilities as a leader. Imagine that you are every bit as successful as you want to be. Feel it and see it.

Keep imagining yourself in the future, and be as specific as possible in your observations. Where exactly are you? Who is your clientele? What are you doing? Who are you interfacing with? What does work look like? How big is it? How are you feeling? Why do you want to be exactly where you are? What is the bigger impact you are having?

Draw a picture of yourself and your surroundings five years from now. Draw the elements you see, feel, and hear. Use as many colours as you want and be as detailed as possible. This is the value of having a vision board.

Step 3: Sum up your vision and mission.

Write responses to the following questions:

How can you sum up your vision and mission as a leader?

What are the things you ultimately want to achieve? Who do you want to be?

What do you want to do?

What is the impact you would like to have and how would you like to be perceived?

What will need to happen in order for you to feel proud of your progress as a leader in five years time?

Now, take everything—the envisioning, writing, drawing, dreaming—and use the language and imagery to write your own vision and mission statement. Give yourself as many drafts as you need to refine it. Remember it should express the values that you would like to live and work by, and that above all you must feel excited and inspired by it when you read it aloud.

Review your vision and mission statement.

As your view of yourself and the future changes, it is important that you review, update and refine your vision and mission statement at least once every six months.

If you feel really inspired, you may even want to expand it with more detail and turn it into a personal development plan.

So get scribbling and imagine how nice it will be to start out in January with a clear roadmap for where you want to go and how to get there!

A woman seeking to find balance between career and family work values could go about the task like this:

- I will seek to balance career and family as best as I can since both are important to me.

- My home will be a place where I and my family, friends and guests find joy, comfort, peace and happiness. I will seek to create a clean and orderly environment yet liveable and comfortable.

- I will be wise in choosing what I eat, read, see and do at home.

- I will teach my children to love, to learn, to enjoy a laugh, and to develop their unique talents.

- I will be a self-starting individual who exercises initiative in accomplishing my life goals.

- I will be proactive with opportunities and situation and not just reactive.

- I will always try to keep free from addictives and destructive habits. I will develop habits that free me from old labels and limits and will expand capabilities and choices.

- My money will be my servant and not my master.

- I will spend less than I earn and regularly save and invest part of my income.

- I will use what money and talents I have to make life more enjoyable for others through service and charitable giving.'

Here are a few mission statements that could inspire you to write yours.

1. To be an amazing friend who is always there.

2. To be a great writer that the world would love to read and learn from.

3. To be a master of the internet and allow the world to come together.

4. To be an explorer and find something wonderful to share with the world where ever I go.

5. To be a wise and inspiring teacher to the young future leaders of the world.

6. To be a super entrepreneur and bring wealth and value to those I serve.

You do truly serve people from top down and maybe you could be the next female billionaire of African descent like Folorunsho Alakija or Christy Walton, who inherited a stake in retailer Wal-Mart, with FORBES estimating her networth to be $41.7 billion. Now, it's time for a game. Why don't you create a vision board? It's a wonderful way to bond as a family.

Let's get creative!

Activity

To get started, you'll need these supplies:

Poster board

A big stack of different magazines. You can get them at libraries, hair salons and doctor's offices. Make sure you find lots of different types. Don't limit your options.

Glue or a glue stick.

Before you begin your vision board, you will also need to set the right mood. Set aside very prejudice. It does not matter where in your life's journey you are now. Remember that you are about to create the life you would enjoy living. Finally, put on soft music (my favourite music is 'Imagine me-Kirk Franklin').

Five steps to your vivid vision board

Step 1: Go through your magazines and tear the images from them. Do not glue yet!

Have lots of fun cutting and making a pile of images, words and phrases.

Whatever grabs your attention on the headlines should join the pile

Step 2: Time to go through the images and begin to lay your favourites on the board. Discard any images that no longer feel right.

This step is where your intuition comes in. As you lay the pictures on the board, you'll get a sense of how the board should be laid out. For instance, what I do and encourage my clients to do is to have different themes on the board. For example: Health, job, Travel, home, spirituality, relationships and finance. Or you just fold the board into a book that tells a story.

Step 3: Glue everything onto the board. Add your own words. Markers are great for this.

Step 4: Leave space in the very centre of the vision board for a fantastic photo of yourself where you look radiant and happy. Paste yourself right at the centre of your board. This helps you live the moments you have described in your board. (this is optional but I advice it).

Step 5: Time to hang your vision board in a place where you will see it constantly. Mine is right at the wall facing my bed. It is the first thing I see once I wake up.

1. The 'sure' vision board.

Select this vision board if:

- You're very clear about your desires.
- You want to change your environment or surroundings.
- There is a specific thing you want to manifest in your life. (i.e. a new baby, or starting a business).

With your clear desire in mind, set out looking for the exact pictures that portray your vision.

I remembered when I wanted to have a baby girl as my second child. I started buying baby clothes, had baby girl pictures around, was always seeing baby girls with their mums, and I always offer to carry them. I was fuelling my vision.

I ended up having a baby. It was a boy! I found it both heartbreaking and hilarious at the same time. Despite this temporary 'set-back', I kept the vision alive until about four years afterwards, my daughter finally emerged.

So, keep the vision alive. Although it may be delayed, it will surely happen.

If you want to start your own business, find images that capture the idea for you. If you want to lose some weight then find before and after pictures. Following the five steps above, create your vision board out of these images.

2. 'Not-so-sure' Vision Board

Select this vision board if:

- You're not sure what exactly you want
- You have suffered a loss or just feeling low.

- You have a vision of what you want, but are uncertain about it in some way.

- You know you want change but don't know how it's possible.

Go through each magazine. Tear out images that delight you.

Don't question your impulse. Just keep going through the magazines. If it's a picture of a Ferrari that jumps at you, cut it out. Or one with a spa resort. Just have fun and be open. Then, as you go through Step 2 above, hold that same openness, but ask yourself what this picture might mean. What is it telling you about you? Choosing pictures strictly by instinct could end up revealing some hidden passion and teach you a lot more about yourself.

3. The 'Theme' Vision Board

Select this vision board if:

- You are working with one particular area of your life. For instance, work and family.

- It's an event with a cycle (e.g., birthdays, New Year Eve, Newly wed, New career etc.)

How to Make a Vision Board for a Theme

The only difference between this vision board and the others is that this one has clear parameters and intent. Before you begin the vision board, take a moment to hold the intent and the theme in mind. When you choose pictures, they will be in alignment with the theme. You can do the Theme Vision Board on smaller pages, like a page in your journal.

Some Things to Remember About Vision Boards

You can use a combination of all three types of vision boards as you create. Sometimes you might start out doing one kind, and then your intuition takes over and shifts into a whole different mode. That's called creativity. It doesn't matter how you make a vision board. Once the creativity is there, just roll with it. Your vision board might change as you are go along.

Make a Vision Journal

Another option is to use these same principles in a big sketch book. Get a large sketch book and keep an on-going vision journal. This is especially effective if you're going through many transitions in your life.

To continually have highly motivated and committed staff members, an organization must strive to know the individual staff's vision and mission in life and formulate career paths within the organization to help them achieve their goals. If I know working for your organization is helping me fulfil my life's vision and mission, I will lend all my energy to ensure the organization achieves its goals too.

Here are examples of different CEOs and their mission statements.

1. DENISE MORRISON, CEO OF CAMPBELL SOUP COMPANY

    To serve as a leader, live a balanced life, and apply ethical principles to make a significant difference.

2. OPRAH WINFREY, FOUNDER OF OWN, THE OPRAH WINFREY NETWORK

    To be a teacher. And to be known for inspiring my students to be more than they thought they could be.

In an issue of *O Magazine*, Winfrey recalls watching her grandmother churn butter and wash clothes in a cast-iron pot in the yard. A small voice inside of her told her that her life would be about more than hanging clothes on a line. She eventually realized she wanted to be a teacher, but 'I never imagined it would be on TV,' she writes. What a world of difference it makes!

3.   AMANDA STEINBERG, FOUNDER OF DAILY WORTH.COM

To use my gifts of intelligence, charisma and serial optimism to cultivate the self-worth and net-worth of women around the world.

Steinberg launched DailyWorth in 2009 to help women build wealth. Since then, she's grown her site to more than 1 million subscribers. 'I believe financially empowered women are the key to world peace,' she says.

There you go!

Activity

Write down your personal statement and keep it where you see it daily. Let it form the basis upon which you make daily decisions.

Chapter 6

PASSION FOR PURPOSE

Anyone can dabble, but once you've made that commitment, your blood has that particular thing in it, and it's very hard for people to stop you.

—Bill Cosby

When my friends, colleagues and clients describe me, it sounds like this 'You are so passionate' and 'it is infectious.'

Have you been described this way? If not, then we have a task to get you there quickly.

I believe life is short and should be lived on purpose, enjoying every second.

Passion is one of the main ingredients you must possess as a female to succeed in any endeavour and especially as a leader. It is contagious.

So, let's talk about passion.

Passion is that strong affection or enthusiasm for an object, concept or project.

My passion has always been to lead in whatever venture I find myself in.

It is that inner drive that helps you overcome obstacles or turn them into stepping stones to reach higher grounds.

In the year 2008, working in corporate Nigeria as a business development manager, having the leadership responsibility of over 65 staff and overseeing the operation and profitability of a region coupled with being a full time wife and mother to two boys.

Sounds like a lot, doesn't it? Yes, as a female you have much more in you than you could ever imagine.

There was an annual Nigerian Bankers' football league organized by Media Visions, which had been massively successful and entertaining. It was the boys' games and all ladies come out to support.

However, I got wind of the information that the 2008 event will incorporate athletics.

I wanted to do something more! I suddenly saw myself winning a gold medal, so I decided to pursue that.

There were huddles to overcome.

The major one was to convince the committee to present me before the management as a worthy candidate, and as the only female attempting to break into 'the boys' club for the first time.

Secondly, to seek approval from the management to invest in additional sponsorship especially for a woman well known as a high flier within the organization. I bet the image I have created is that of a no-nonsense-go-getter and participating in sports was far from anyone's mind.

Thirdly, ensure my work as a business development manager continues unencumbered during preparations.

Lastly, overcoming limiting beliefs (Yes, I was a mother of 2 boys then, who I gave birth to through the caesarean section and I had a bit of struggles getting my belle area back under control. I am sure women-folks can relate to this).

Here is one of my favourite quotes:

> *Exceptionality requires creativity fuelled by passion coupled with hardwork.*
>
> —Sheun Olotu-Oke

Never be afraid to be first. You may just be the one to blaze the trail for others coming after you.

Yes, It may never be easy but it is super rewarding.

To forge ahead I had to PLAN AHEAD. This important acronym was popularized by John Maxwell, and it has helped me and will be of tremendous value to you too if applied.

P- Predetermine a course of action

L- Layout goals

A- Adjust priorities

N- Notify key personnel

A- Allow time for acceptance

H- Head into action

E- Expect problems

A- Always point to the successes

D- Daily review plan

I had a meeting with my family and presented my plan to them. My children were ecstatic! Mum will be participating in the 100 meter and 200 meter dash and winning two medals!

My sons agreed to be my running partners (I have an adopted son who just became a teenager and my first biological son was over 5 years at the time).

I started working out 30 minutes daily, which meant I had to wake up 30 minutes earlier then my normal 5.30am wake-up time. My husband took me through the warm-up routines.

I would get the children ready for school and set out with my chauffer to the office. Then after setting the order of work for the office, I would send out mail to the committee. Bombarding them with not just e-mails but calls. I was building a good rapport and letting them know it is an investment well worth making.

My weekends were devoted to more training. The footballers had a paid coach, but my husband had to assume the role of unpaid coach. Hurray! After much persistence and pestering, we got the approval for sponsorship! But as for me, there was no allowance for my training kit whereas all the footballers had new branded kits.

Ladies, it may be the men's world like the general saying, but you can always get what you want out of them if only you will not take 'No' for an answer.

I could not be deterred. I personally funded my kit (this was later refunded).

The competition day came. It was a beautiful sunny day. The whole Diamond bank athletic crew entered into the stadium (one woman crew—smiling). My family, hundreds of DB staff and the football team were all part of the crowd. The stalls were filled with men, women and children waving and cheering.

The marching band's music boomed from the sides. Then, I saw my competitors (about 15 financial institutions registered to participate). My heart skipped a beat. 'Sheun, this is the moment...Are you sure you want to do this? What if you mess up?' These were the thoughts going through my mind.

I was the only management staff and by far the most matured. All the others were fresh university graduates: slim, trim and fit. They were tickled pink when they realized who I was. Of course, I had to give them my business cards for further contacts.

I almost lost my cool but my passion and determination kept me on track. We all lined up on the tracks.

'All set' Ready?' called out the official, and boom! The gun fired and we were off.

The race started. I could feel the wind rushing towards and enveloping me. My heart raced faster than my legs. I could hear the cheers coming from all sides. I could see the finishing line, and I could see only one person levelling up with me. Finally, the end of the first race! I did it!

Although I didn't win the gold, I won two silver medals for 100m and 200m.

My organization was super proud! My husband came to do a celebration dance with me. My children were proud. Mum had done it!

Yes, yet another trophy to my passion that pushes past pain.

Did I struggle with differing emotions and challenges? Absolutely!

Your strength of character is built up following your passion. Above that all is the reward and the confidence you build becoming the person that you were created to be.

Award presented by Uk Eke - Ex. Dir
(Now MD First Bank Nigeria Ltd)

Elements that Make Passion Work

- Find a purpose.
- Set your agenda by determining how the purpose is to be achieved.
- Get your support team in place.
- Make bold and talk about it so you are accountable.
- Do what you said you would.
- Set your expectation 10 times higher.

Les Brown said 'Shoot for the moon and if you miss, you will still be among the stars.'

Remember: Teach this to your children. It is your duty to study your children and to pass the passion knowledge to them.

If you thought this was illuminating, you'll be blown away by the concepts I will share with you in the next chapter! All you need do is flip the page.

Chapter 7

EMPLOYEE-PRENEURSHIP

Employee-preneurship is an abridged name between employee and entrepreneur.

I first heard this word from one of my mentors—multimillionaire Dani Johnson.

I was intrigued immediately. Why? Now I could understand why I was able to advance quickly in my career. I was an employee-preneur!

Let's first take a look at who an 'employee' is.

An employee is someone who takes on the job, routinely comes in to work and goes home. They are the ones who push the paper or crunch the numbers and collect the pay check. They do the bare minimum. Take every possible break with eyes on the clock, ever ready to leave at the dot of time-whether the job gets done or not. They do what is asked of them, and no more. They do often cut corners and look for the easy way out. They use peer pressure to hold others back by 'talking' ambitious co-workers out of doing more because it makes them look bad. They revel in gossips keeping others from achieving and creating a bad office environ. They think they have paid their dues and never have to work hard again.

Does that sound like someone you know? Absolutely!

What about an entrepreneur?

An entrepreneur has invested in their company and wants it to succeed. Why? Their profits come from solving clienteles' problems. Most employers are looking for workers who exemplify these traits.

Qualities of entrepreneurs

- They take initiative.
- They are constantly working on their personal skill levels so they can keep up in the competitive marketplace of today's world.
- They have positive mental attitudes
- They work under constraints but never allow themselves to be constrained.
- They have a sense of ownership
- They have great amount of self-esteem and self-confidence.
- They are dedicated.
- They use feedback and continually improve on products and services.
- They have great survival instinct and are adaptable.

What if an employee could exhibit all the qualities of the entrepreneur and more?

I am sure they would be irreplaceable! That is who I was as an employee and highly recommend that you be like this too.

An employee-preneur is someone who, although they receive a salary, is willing to take on the full responsibilities of making the organization she works for super successful. She earns more with time and becomes the 'talk-about' of others. She not only follows instructions, but where she naturally sees a need, she takes charge.

Steps to becoming an Employee-preneur

1. **Pre-determine the industry you want to work in; research and know all the requirements; get ready to give it your best; and distinguish yourself from the rest of the pack.**

   For example, before leaving university, I knew I wanted to work in financial services. I guess what first informed my decision was seeing professionally dressed ladies working within this industry.

   They look well and are very well paid. Writing this makes me smile because what we really do see and get attracted to, we end up becoming.

   I decided to start studying the industry, getting to know the top players, their challenges, continuous training opportunities within, career progressions. e.t.c. I took time to visit some.

   Before I was out of the university, I knew exactly where I wanted to work. It was to be the Zenith Bank.

   Whilst still in my final year, my fiancé, Stephen (now my husband), encouraged me to start studying for the aptitude tests (e.g., the GMAT-Graduate Management Admission Test).

He said, 'Sheun, no more novels. The GMAT becomes your only novel henceforth until you get your dream job.'

So there I was with rigorous coursework, final year project in progress, lectures and additional GMAT work.

Becoming the best and getting your choice never really comes easy. John C Maxwell says, 'You have to give up to go up.'

What are you willing to give up to achieve your dream or vision?

There is always an 'opportunity cost' to your choices.

2. **Be ready to overcome obstacles.**

Obstacles are what hinders or obstructs you from achieving your pre-determined goals or objectives. The presence of obstacles does not mean you are on the wrong path, but in reality, they are what test your tenacity or focus on achieving your goals.

Why do we have to go through interviews or aptitude tests? It's simply because the employer wants the person with the best fit to achieve the organizational goals. My goal of getting into the financial sector required me to prove myself fit among thousands of others.

The first obstacle I experienced in getting my first professional job was the area of proving that I was out of school on my Curriculum Vitae.

I knew there would be lots more CVs going to all the employers once all University graduates are out of school and maximum tendency for lots to be lost n the maze, and more so, stiffer competition due to numbers.

To get a head-start, I submitted my own CV to the head

offices of all the major financial institutions of my interest, documenting as follows:

My anticipated result: 2nd class upper division (in view)

In the area specified for 'availability for immediate employment,' I wisely wrote 'AWAITING NYSC.' In the area specified for NYSC details, I wrote 'AWAITING NYSC.' NYSC is the acronym used in Nigeria to represent the 1-year compulsory voluntary work required of all university graduates. Without presenting this certificate, employers are under statutory regulations not to employ you. Even if you studied abroad, as long as you would still desire to work within Nigeria, you must do the service. It stands for National Youth Service Corps.

To anyone that picks up my CV, there must have been a thought, 'Hmmm, who is this lady?'

Upon graduating and completing the three week NYSC intensive camp (compulsory military grooming before members are sent out to different organizations to work), many financial institutions and different employers came to hold recruitment workshops on my campus and invite participants for aptitude tests.

Some corps members were sent to different establishments pre-determined by the NYSC body, but some who had passed and gotten engaged through the aptitude test routes were posted to the establishments that requested for them.

I was first posted to the Ministry of Agriculture (first hurdle) and spent about 3 months there before finally getting to my pre-determined organization, Zenith Bank!

There is nothing that beats the power of you knowing exactly what you want, going for it and refusing to settle for less.

So many graduates had to go searching for their dream jobs after the NYSC program but as for me, I was already where I wanted to be.

My second hurdle: I got pregnant during the NYSC year! Myself and my fiancé had planned to get married as long as one of us was gainfully employed (this is one of the values of having a personal vision and mission). We knew we wanted to be with each other forever.

My organization did not know how to handle it! Even as a full staff member, you are not entitled to a maternity leave until after you have spent two years with the establishment. It was an unwritten law that nobody really dared to flout.

Here I was, still in voluntary service, although having gone through the full recruitment process which required four interview stages with the ultimate interview with the CEO then, Jim Ovia, yet I had broken the unwritten law!

Everyone except me knew that I 'blew my chance at a dream job'!

After the compulsory one year service, all NYSC staff was given automatic employment except one person...ME!

Heartbroken, I went home and had my baby on that beautiful 21st day of October 2003. No job, but I had the most amazing gift ever! A bouncing baby boy.

I have always been a people person. One of the greatest books I ever read as a teenager and young leader was *How to Make Friends and Influence People* by Dale Carnegie. If you have never read it, I strongly recommend it to you and your children.

I had made lots of friends within the system, including some of the managers at the bank. Not to blow my trumpet, but I was an employee-preneur, indeed!

I was not the only heart-broken person within the system. Lots of people were on the lookout for me too.

I promised to keep in touch with the head of human resources who also happened to be another powerful woman (in real fact, the HR department was 99% female).

I took my baby to the head office for a visit and the whole of the HR department lit up! 'Sheun's beautiful baby has come to work!' It was awesome seeing the connecting effect that taking my baby for a visit had. My baby was then 1 month old (he now stands taller than his mum at just over 11 years).

The head of human resources asked me to stay in touch and come for a chat when baby turned 3 months.

I did, but stories started building. I was asked if I had started applying to other establishments. I said 'No.' I knew exactly where I wanted to work, and it was at the bank.

Compressing the rest of the story, I remained persistent; even at the face of massive obstacles, I kept listening for relevant information, I was prepared to have a heart to heart talk with the CEO himself until I heard the HR department management had changed to another amazing leader, Lara Alagbada. I persisted and finally on the day my baby became 6 months old, I was back to my dream job!

The greatest tip on surmounting your obstacle: KEEP YOUR EYES ON THE GOAL.

Lara Alagbada (Zenith Bank Plc HR Director) presenting me with a certificate of completion at the training school.

3. **Seek to always add value to yourself to prepare you for advancement.**

Several organizations have robust training packages to help forward-looking employee-preneurs achieve their personal goals.

For example, working with the Imperial College NHS Trust, I was able to train as a certified project and risk manager (PRINCE2, MoR) among other courses.

Although I was managing a team of 9 staff, who had spent between 9 years to 25 years in the same roles, none was ready to step out of her comfort zone to take on such courses. I was in total shock to realize that a young lady or woman could continue a routine job for so many years without aspiring to take on more!

You must invest your time in attending courses, seminars, training and so on, and not just the ones provided by your organization, but also the ones that can help you be a better you.

I offer free leadership courses to add value to you. Book online at www.sheunoke.com

If you are not increasing in knowledge, you are decreasing in person.

4. **Volunteer for more.**

There are times that your employers need to organize events or programmes that are not specified on your job description. e.g. volunteering to tackle social issues.

Benefits include positive effects on brand value and reputation, and the bringing to life of corporate values.

Employee volunteering builds networks through collaboration with other businesses, engages companies and suppliers and can increase a company's chances in tendering processes.

Of people who took part in employee volunteering, statistics reveal that 87% reported an improved perception of their employer and 82% reported feeling more committed to their employer

70% of employee volunteers reported developing their time management, communication, influencing, decision-making and leadership skills.

81% of community partners had an improved perception of the employer they worked with and 99% would recommend the company to others.

The support of employee volunteers can make a real difference to local communities. Many community organisations, groups and charities are experiencing a huge increase in demand for their services at the same time as being faced with cuts in public sector funding that have left them struggling to continue providing much-needed services.

So, get involved!

5. **Be autonomous.**

An employer wants you to get the job done without extensive hand-holding. So, get to understand your job descriptions, fashion your deliverables out with your line manager, get them broken down to daily tasks and learn to prioritise. The value of an employee-preneur is to know what needs to be done at what time and get it done. Period!

6. **Be energetic.**

Employees who come into work fresh and energetic everyday are going to out-produce workers who think negatively and easily burn-out when they encounter defeat. Upbeat and optimistic employees create a working environment that is unique, spawns new ideas and, just as important is enjoyable for the other people involved. I have always been accused of being 'so full of energy.' Yes, I love it! You make your organization into the best place on earth.

7. **Be Confident.**

Confidence produces results and encourages you to take on challenges that others shy away from. Since you are working in the organization that you pre-selected, getting to know all about your products and services and knowing how to present it to your clientele to solve their problem, will always give you an edge.

Confidence is an outward show of your internal belief in yourself and your abilities. The best companies are highly confident in their abilities to provide a superior product or service and this belief spawns a culture of improvement and client confidence.

8. **Detail Oriented.**

Attention to detail is crucial or mistakes will be made within your company. Be detail-oriented by taking pride in your work. Ensure you get the job done.

9. **Modest.**

The most sought after employees shout their value not through their words, but rather through their work. They are humble, don't need to pump themselves up in front of others and quietly out-produce those who do.

10. **Be Hard Working.**

Nothing great is accomplished easily. Nothing great is accomplished via being a '9 to 5 type of employee.' Rather, the foundation of any effective organization lies in its ability to recruit results oriented, hard working employees who execute. And that makes you 'Irreplaceable'!

11. **Be presentable.**

Appropriate dressing helps you look and feel great. You can easily tell who successful employee-preneurs are because they are well packaged at all times and when dealing with clients, they are able to represent their organization as professional and organized.

Chapter 8

ENTREPRENEURSHIP:
THE ART OF PROFITING FROM
PROBLEMS SOLVED

We have explored the channel of being the best employee you could be which is becoming an 'Employee-preneur.'

Now is the time to step up the tempo and introduce you to what could ultimately help you make more difference in the world at large.

Remember, someone gave you a job? And you earn a salary/wage? What if that person had not created an enterprise? How would you earn a living?

About 5 years ago, one of my mentors and an international business owner- Boye Abe, defined a job for me, and I am sure you would find it fascinating once you read it.

Just

Over

Broke

You should be smiling now if you are an employee or employee-preneur because you understand what that really means.

Most live from paycheck to paycheck. A salary is designed to help you meet your needs and no matter how much you earn, your living costs rise up to match up and the cycle goes on and on.

Have you ever felt frustrated by this or know a friend who is? Then you are just about to get an antidote!

Entrepreneurship! I am sure you would have heard this word several times and may understand a bit about what it represents.

I got to know about the concept before getting to hear about the word though. The concept from where I grew up is simply termed 'Business'. My mum was a business woman. She told me, 'Sheun, I started working at age 16 plus at the Ministry of Agriculture.' What a coincidence! I am just realizing that this same ministry was where I was first posted as a Youth Corps member before I was able to conclude my paperwork to get my dream bank job. She continued, 'I loved the salary but there was something that kept tugging at my heart, always echoing, there has got to be more than this to life.'

'I had a mental picture of my ideal job and here was my list,' mum said. 'No boss. No alarm clocks No compromises. Time with family. The ability to take my children along to the office without feeling guilty. No educational requirement. No politics (I hated one of my obnoxious bosses)! No discrimination. But I knew that was a dream. So I started creating an exit plan. I started a part-time business of supplying men's undergarments (I knew I could give them a price without expecting them to haggle).This grew and my confidence with it. Then on turning 21 years old, I decided to take the plunge to becoming an entrepreneur. No regrets whatsoever,' she concluded.

Although she is of blessed memories now, this conversation was timeless.

She started her full time foray into entrepreneurship by supplying undergarments to her former colleagues, went on to office supplies, and ultimately became a successful restaurateur.

'An entrepreneur is someone who can take any idea, whether it be a product and/or service, and have the skill set, will and courage to take extreme risk to do whatever it takes to turn that concept into reality and not only bring it to market, but make it a viable product and/or service that people want or need,' says MJ Gottlieb, co-founder of Hustle Branding.

That about sums it up!

The Statistics

The Guardian reports that the UK unemployment figures showed that women were losing their jobs at a disproportionately greater rate than men. Of the 2.67 million people who are unemployed, 1.12 million are women – the highest number for 25 years. One factor is that the number of women in the labour market has increased over recent decades.

'In previous recessions like the early 1980s, female unemployment figures weren't nearly as high because there were fewer women in work to lose their jobs,' says Graeme Cooke, Associate Director of the Institute for Public Policy Research. 'It reflects the fact that women's levels of participation have gone up. But more recently it is to do with job losses in the public sector where women disproportionately work.'

Women make up around 65% of the public sector, and are represented even more highly in some areas, such as local government, where 75% of workers are female. 'When you look ahead to the 710,000 jobs that will be going from the public sector 2015. that is going to disproportionately impact on women,' says a spokesperson for union Unison. 'It is especially worrying because those years of their career are really crucial in building up their pension contribution. It's not just a short-term problem of being jobless, it's the risk that they will be unable to make up their lost pension contributions and then face a much lower standard of living in retirement and potentially greater reliance on state benefits.' He continued.

In the USA, 6.5% of the females accounting for over 24,000,000 are unemployed!

In Africa, for example Mali has 85% females of their Tertiary/ University graduates being unemployed!

The statistics may keep worsening as the Tertiary institutions keep churning out trained employees with not enough people looking to create the jobs.

Eric Worre, the CEO of Network marketing Pro analysed the employee market progression over the last century. The cycle looks like this: Go to school to learn how to be an employee; find a company that will employ you; work for that company for 30 to 40 years; and retire with a pension to take care of you in old age.

This has ended up failing progressively with the promise of a 'good pension' going down the drain. Some pension funds were actually lost through the recession. In short, over the past decade or so, people have realized that the loyalty promised in times past is now non-existent, so a different process has evolved:

Go to school and learn to be an employee; find a company that employs you; switch companies for various economical and political reasons every three to five years; and find you can't retire comfortably after 30 to 40years, so keep working.

Does this ring a bell for you?

Entrepreneurship is the breakaway, and it is by far the most important way to be financially free and wealthy. The females need to do more of this to stand firm as leaders solving the worlds' problems.

Most successful entrepreneurs follow comparable patterns and share similar basic characteristics. Hundreds of online articles and published books claim to know the secret of success in business, but for the most part, they boil down to the same major points.

Passion, perseverance and a positive attitude tend to set successful entrepreneurs apart. Cultivating these attributes requires an innate skill set and some tips to get started.

If you want to be a millionaire, go help a million people!

I have made up my mind to help billions of people, starting from you. I can't wait to hear you share your stories of victories with me.

Steps to Becoming an Entrepreneur

1. Spot a Need and Solve a Problem

One of my successful business venture as an undergraduate came out of spotting a need (so do not wait for graduation day to start your venture!). I was in my third year of study whilst my fiancé was in his fourth year. Typically as Agricultural students, (We both studied Agricultural economics and Extension as our first degree) the fourth year is spent on the University farm projects. The location was far removed from 'civilization'. I noticed that feeding on the farm was a bit challenging for the students numbering over 100 persons.

They would have to travel one hour into town to get any decent food and another hour back. Most ended up not eating at all or just snacked and I could notice that this affected their productivity and mood.

I watched this for over 3 weeks, and then suddenly, an idea occurred to me. What if I could provide sumptuous and affordable meals for them right there on the farm, saving them time and energy? (I grew as a mini restaurateur, as my mum ran one of the most popular restaurants in my town then:

Ade-royal restaurants). I asked for my fiancé's opinion and he seemed to love the idea. I had a mini survey done and the feedback was positive.

Voilà! Sheun to the rescue! I started my mobile restaurant, which was highly profitable. I spotted a need, I solved a problem, clientele was happy, I got richer. Win-win situation.

Ziglar Ziglar said, 'If you help enough people get what they want, you will get everything that you want.'

2. Fine-tune an Existing Product or Service

You don't necessarily have to do something revolutionary or brand-new to be successful. You just have to be better at something than your competitors. Who are your competitors? What is the edge you are offering your clientele?

Jasmine Lawrence, the CEO of EDEN Bodyworks, became an entrepreneur whilst trying to find a solution to a personal tragedy.

As a child, she was confident and very outgoing, however, at age 11, trying out a hair relaxer on her afro hair, all her hair totally fell out. This totally affected her self-esteem so she was on a crusade to find natural ingredients to help her hair grow back. She found several online and created her own edge by making different natural hair concussions. Fast-forward, she is estimated to have made over $3 million providing her solutions to others.

Do something you love.

You will likely be more successful if you do something you know and love. Going into might make your business very marketable, but if your heart's not in it you won't have the energy to keep yourself going.

Allyson Ames, CEO of Wonderland Bakery, had the love for baking. As a 5year old, she loved creating several pastries and was full of imagination about amazing pastries. By the time she turned 13years old , she had collected an impressive amount of cookery books. In just her early twenties, she is estimated to have made over $2.5 millions in sales all stemmed from a dream of a 5 year old!

If you're having trouble thinking of an idea, create a list of things about your target market, such as places they shop and things they purchase. Narrow the list down to about three items, keeping cost, manufacturing time, and popularity in mind. Find the easiest, most realistic product you can offer. For example, I offer image coaching for top executives between the ages of 24-65 which naturally led me into weight loss products to help my clientele shape up. There is nothing that boosts a woman's self esteem than getting into her dream dress!

3. Research

The key to starting a business is to know whether there is a demand for your product or service. Is what you can offer something that is not being done as well as it could be? Is it a need that doesn't have enough supply to support demand?

Analyse the risk. Entrepreneurship is always a game of risk and reward, but often the risk is greater (especially in the beginning).

Take stock of all your assets and figure out how much money (and time and energy) you actually have to invest.

In addition to considering your savings, credit, and other sources of capital, consider how long you can afford to go without making a profit. Small businesses are rarely profitable immediately; can you afford to not draw a salary for perhaps several months or even a few years?

4. Present your Findings

If you have done good market research, you should be able to talk in specifics about your chosen industry or field, your target consumer market, and your projected market share. This section should be as detailed as possible, as it needs to convince investors that you know what you're doing.

One of the mistakes many beginning entrepreneurs make is failing to narrow their target market and trying to sell to too wide an audience. While it's tempting to believe that everyone needs and will love your product or service, the reality is that they won't. It's okay to start small.

Include and organogram even if your company is only you at this point, use this section to provide information on who owns your company, what their responsibilities are, and how you will structure your business as it expands. (Will you have a board of directors? How will your employees be organized?) Investors want to see that you have thought about the future of your company.

5. Get the word out!

It's time to let the world know what you have to offer by advertising. How do you reach your target audience?

Remember, sales is 10% content, 90% marketing.

Get a good system that can help you manage your clientele especially for repeat buying. Some small and medium scale businesses use Infusionsoft which has a total customer management system.

The internet has made doing business more interesting as you can reach the world from your very living room or anywhere at all from your laptop.

Several platforms to sell online are available so you could start no matter how small (e.g., eBay selling, Amazon, Etsy, Shopify, etc.).

6. Network

Attend trade and industry shows in your field and talk with exhibitors. Join relevant professional associations. Build a strong social network with other entrepreneurs, both online (using social media and professional sites like Linkedin) and in person.

Attending networking events such as local fairs hosted by your chamber of commerce is a great way to connect with other entrepreneurs in your area. These connections can provide you with support, ideas, and opportunities.

Be generous to others. Don't consider networking with other entrepreneurs only in terms of what they can give you. If you offer advice, ideas, and support to others, they will be more likely to want to help you as well. Nobody likes to feel exploited.

Pay close attention to other people's ideas. Even if you're in direct competition with someone, you can probably still learn from them. You can learn from others' mistakes as well as their successes, but only if you listen to them.

A shinning example of female entrepreneurship is Nigeria's wealthiest woman, Folorunsho Alakija.

She is estimated to be worth $2.6 billion by FORBES. What company would pay you salary of that amount! This woman did not have a University degree.

The Nigerian businesswoman explained to the students that while a University degree is important and can significantly improve one's prospects in life, hard work and persistence were the most crucial tools for success.

Alakija pursued secretarial studies and fashion design as a young woman in London, and then returned to Nigeria to work as a secretary in a Merchant bank. She subsequently founded Supreme Stitches, a tailoring outfit that catered to upscale clientele including Nigeria's fashionable former first lady Maryam Babangida. In 1993, she acquired an oil prospecting license which granted her a lucrative block in Nigeria's coastal waters. Her company, Famfa Oil, now holds a 60% stake in the oil field. She is also the founder of The Rose of Sharon Foundation, which provides support to orphans and widow.

Mark Victor Hansen in his book ' Richest kids in America' documented some amazing stories of young people that started their entrepreneurship journey earlier in life.

For example: Martina Butler, 18yr old creator of an internet based radio show-emogirltalk is estimated to have made over $1.8million turning her love for music and fashion into a worthy business.

What Akiane Kramirak, a 14year old who turned her love for arts and poetry into a thriving million dollar business?

Entrepreneurship has high returns but you have to be ready to give it all it takes to work and it is never too early to start.

Accelerate your entry into Entrepreneurship

If you want to get started quickly on your entrepreneurship venture, and receive all the support you could get especially on mindset? Then you must consider joining a multilevel marketing/Direct sales company.

The multi-level marketing industry is evolving and has boasted of creating several female millionaires in the past decade. The industry is estimated have made $167 billion in sales in 2012 alone! Compared to Music industry- $16.5 billion, video gaming industry-$67billion, and organic products industry-$91billion.

40% of this was directly to distributors as commissions.

In a chat with Paula Pritchard, who has put in 35 years at MLM, she told me:

> I was a teacher in the University making a decent income. However, I wanted to buy a house but the money was just not enough. That was when I was introduced to network marketing. It was a learning and growing process for me. Yes, I failed a little but kept at it until I became massively successful.

Among other things, it is essential to consider the following: the benefits of network marketing/direct sales where industry analysis is done for you and products and services are already fine-tuned. Other benefits include already having a system of sales and customer relationships in place. In short, the logistics headache is all taken care of! The earning potential is unlimited and there is no gender pay-rate. Whatever a male earns in commissions is what a female will.

Robert Kiyosaki, *The New York Times* bestselling author of *Rich Dad Poor Dad* observes:

> *The network marketing industry offers a simple business system for anyone to take control of their financial future.*

So as a lady with different constraints, you can get a hold of your financial future by researching and getting into a company that aligns with your personal vision and mission.

There is nothing that beats the value of word-of-mouth advertisement.

Have you ever asked someone to join Facebook? Yes! That's was how I built a friend list of 5000 plus in less than one year! Was I paid for it? Absolutely not! Ever asked someone to sign up for a Google account? I bet so. What about Twitter?

These companies have built a base of billions of people strictly through referral/word of mouth marketing, and you and I were never paid.

However, the multi-level marketing companies pay you for using their products and referring same to your network. As long as there is a product or service provided by these companies, they are no scams nor are they pyramids.

Be cautious however. It is not a get-rich-quick system but you can get really rich.

The more the products you sell in your organization, and the more leaders you breed, the more income you make.

Your success depends on many factors, including:

- Your commitment to dedicating a minimum of 5 to 7 hours per week to the success of your business.

- An initial start up cost ranging £50-£200 (in the UK there is a strict regulation that does not permit a resident to spend more than £200 in the first 7 days of joining a direct sales or MLM company). The cost may be more in other countries.

- The ability to continue to financially support your business (out of pocket)

- Your ability to be coachable and willingness to follow through on the required tasks and actions.

If you want to be involved in this sector, you must decide to be a professional. It takes some learning. Looking to get information on how to get started or improve your results in MLM? Email me at sheun@sheunoke.com.

Chapter 9

SPEAKING FOR INFLUENCE: THE ART OF WORD-SHAPING

He who wants to persuade should put his trust not in the right argument, but in the right word. The power of sound has always been greater than the power of sense.
—Joseph Conrad

D o you know that the number one fear of a vast majority of the people is Public speaking!

If I ask you to come in front of 5 people right away to speak about a subject, what will be your first reaction? Will your heart skip a beat? Over 90% will panic and refuse.

It happens to us all including children!

Being able to use words to create desired emotions is a must-have-skill for you as a leader and to succeed in any life endeavour.

Just imagine a head teacher who is highly qualified for his or her job but cannot stand before the governing bodies to speak or present ideas?

What about a sale's person who is afraid of presenting his goods or services to potential clients?

Based on a number of surveys carried out by top organizations like Microsoft, BBC, NACE and others, for skills often deemed indispensably important for career advancement, verbal communication ranks number one, followed closely by written communication.

Now, if you must lead as a woman or girl, you must learn to be comfortable with this skill.

Would you like to know why most people avoid speaking or presenting?

You care too much about what people think or what they would say. What other people think about you is none of your business! Do your best.

Here is a statement that holds true at all times, 'You cannot lead whom you cannot influence.'

No better way to influence anyone than the use of carefully crafted words.

> *Of all the talents bestowed on men, none is so precious as the gift of oratory and anyone who enjoys it wields a power more durable than that of a great King.*
> —Winston Churchill

Imagine yourself entering a room full of 5000 people, speaking and you could feel the whole atmosphere charged with a positive energy created by no other but you. Lives are about to change for the better just because you have spoken as a master! Yes, even you can!

Did I sense you doubting that? Do not. I have got great news for you! Speaking is a learnable skill.

Whether it's speaking to present an idea to a team of 5, or to the management of an organization, or coursework in school, or speaking as a religious group leader, as an entrepreneur, a coach, a trainer?

The best speakers in the world were once bad speakers but they continued learning, practising and re-adjusting until they have gotten 'good'.

I remember my very first stint at public speaking. I was 7 years old and asked to recite a poem at our general school assembly. I had two weeks to prepare. I had learnt the poems by heart, recited before my family so many times that my mum begged me to stop!

I bet everyone in my house knew the poem by heart!

Then the glorious day came. I woke up to the sound of the cock crowing, stretched and smiled. It was all so surreal around but inside me was a wave of excitement that was almost drowning.

I got dressed, had breakfast with my mum and my siblings (dad was working out of town).

Then time to go to school. We set out and as always, I was in a jolly mood- skipping and walking all the way to school.

I got into the class and my classmates called out, 'Go, Sheun go!'

I smiled. Yes! It's the day I had been waiting for.

My class teacher called me to have the last rehearsal before we all trooped out to the assembly.

Unbeknownst to us, a dignitary from the Catholic Church

would be present and my head-teacher wanted to present only the best pupils.

So it was time.

'Ladies and gentlemen, honourable guests, we hereby present the amiable Oluwaseun Olotu, to recite her poem'!

The whole school crowd of over 1000 students cheered!

I bounded up the stage and stood. Looking upon the seas of heads and smiled.

Yes, I was ready!

I opened my mouth...... no sound came! I went totally blank! I froze. All eyes on me.

I stood there for the longest one minute of my life. Sheun, the orator could not utter a word.

My head teacher came to me and smiled kindly. I busted into tears! The whole school started clapping to encourage me as I went off the stage.

Have you ever felt like public speaking is not your thing? Maybe you have had really embarrassing time trying. I have been there too and I promise you, speaking is a learnable skill and I will be taking your hands to walk you through all the landmines so you become a confident speaker, that is ready to boldly lead your team.

Here we go!

7 Levels of Speaker Awareness

There are different levels of speaker awareness and they are divided into seven.

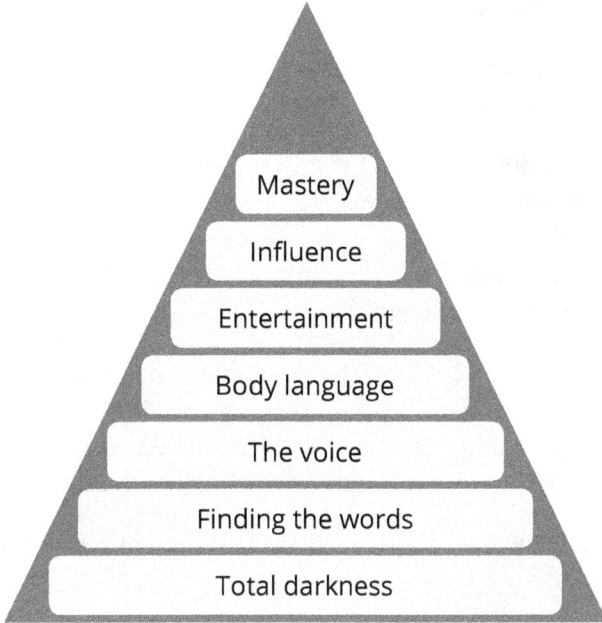

Mastery

Influence

Entertainment

Body language

The voice

Finding the words

Total darkness

Level 1

Total darkness: Ignorance and avoidance. You just want to avoid any form of speaking. If called on you, you would pass on the opportunity to someone else. This level is characterized by fear of failure to deliver. You think that speaking is just for natural speakers. You couldn't be farther from the truth!

Level 2

Finding the words: You were either pulled out by inspiration or pushed by desperation.

For example, preparing for an interview to get your dream job and you were asked to present your idea on a PowerPoint slide.

When speaking, you are mostly preoccupied with what you will say, so you start to panic.

Being in a panicked state shuts down your system and could lead to momentary memory loss.

Imagine having prepared for an interview and ending up not remembering your best examples? It happened to me once on a telephone interview. I had rehearsed all examples for all competencies stated but totally went blank on relating a story for conflict management!

At a level higher, you know the words but you just rattle through your words so you can get through. As a result, your speech has no modulations or inflections nor life. All you want to do is just get your speaking done and disappear from the audience's sight.

At this level you know what to say but the voice has not been fine-tuned.

I can remember some of my old college professors talking on in monotones and all we want them to do is to set us free! A good presentation is more than the words.

Level 3

Voice: Speaking is not just what you say, but how you say it. Your passion shows in your tonality, your volume. Every modulation of your voice has its own effect.

You have to learn to make your audience feel special by connecting with them through your stories.

Sounds and rhythm are important. Knowing when to pause, allowing time for thought and quick reflections to draw your listeners in.

You have to make it feel like an adlib—just like every seasoned speaker- you must learn how to make your listeners believe that you are making up the words right there and then but we all know the truth.

The best speakers in the world practice, practice, practice, until the lines come out as an adlib. The key is to have lots of practice.

Level 4

Body language: This is a non-verbal communication where your thoughts, intents or feelings are expressed by physical behaviour such as stance, facial expressions, gesture, touch or use of space. Are you maintaining eye contacts strategically? Moving with precision? Smiling at the right time?

By your body language, it is easy to tell if you are enjoying yourself or not.

Level 5

Entertainment: Here, your passion is palpable and matches you voice. You have found ways to connect with your audience and your body language is saying ' I enjoy being right here'.

You are not too fussy with your hands and you appear confident and unhurried. You are looking out for your audiences' reaction and you are adjusting effortlessly along the way. You can feel the vibes of your audience. Are they listening? Are you touching their needs? Are they actively listening?

This is higher grounds and you are aware that your speech is all about the audience.

Level 6

Influence: This is possible if only you have built up on the other five. Are the people buying? Are they taking steps you are proffering? What is your purpose for the presentation? It has to be designed in such a way to increase your influence with your audience without sounding condescending.

My mentor, John C Maxwell, is one of the greatest speakers with influence that I know and this is why I chose him above all to

He speaks to fortune 500 companies and has written over 74 books yet when he gives examples, it never feels like he is blowing his own horn.

Why? He has learnt how to appropriately design his speeches to increase his influence whilst focusing on giving his audience the very best experience.

Level 7

Mastery: This is the highest level and here is where you aim to be.

At this level, you have tested your speech material severally, obtained feedback, re-adjusted and retested again. Your speaking becomes unconscious at this level just like you would hold a normal conversation. There are some valuable tools to use to get to this level. Videos and voice recorders.

Record your speech. Watch or listen critically to it. Make necessary adjustments to the errors perceived. Re-record and listen/watch again. Send it to your coach/mentor to get a feedback. Make necessary adjustments by Incorporating the feedback. Repeat the process until you get your desired result.

The value of your personal story can never be undermined. It helps you connect with your audience. Remember, nobody has exactly the same life experiences as you and telling your story helps others identify more with you.

Becoming a master at speaking is a process that takes time but

If you are willing to invest in the process, you will increase your influence as a leader immensely and trust me, the reward is far outweighs the your input at getting 'good.'

There is a massive shortage of female speakers. This is another profession you want to consider.

Activity

1. Can you spot your level now? Write it down.

2. What is your action plan to get to the next level?

3a. Do you presently have a coach? Yes/ No

3b. If your answer to 3a is No, time to contact me at <u>www. sheunoke.com,</u> and I will be more than happy to coach you.

Chapter 10

FAITH

*F*aith is taking the first step even when you can't see the whole stairs.

The concept of faith is world-wide and encompasses the totality of our lives. There is not a single person that succeeded in life without faith.

Faith is the visualization of and belief in the attainment of our desire.

Do you really desire to lead in your field? Or desire it for your children?

Then you have to develop a firm faith.

Faith in what? Faith in yourself, your goal and in the ultimate superior being, who for me is God through Jesus Christ.

My life took a better turn when I took a bold step to let go of depending on just myself.

I remember a dark time in my teenage years. I had gone through terrible emotional turbulence and felt life was not worth living again, so I was depressed and suicidal (This was a shock to my mum when I later revealed it to her well into my 30s). After all, why live if all you are getting is heart aches?

I believe this is a phase that almost all teenagers go through in search of self.

Nic Vujicic, an evangelist and motivational speaker, talked about suicide attempts in the teenagers being as high as 12.8% in Hawaii.

Every single person is created for a specific purpose. Most stumble through life trying to find it and trust me, I did too.

I was in search of something that I couldn't quite describe. Now I know that it is a search for purpose in life.

So if you are a mother, an aunt, grandmother or female mentor, you have a crucial responsibility of helping your young ones discover themselves and faith in God.

I was brought up in a Christian home and have been in the choir since I was 7 years old. There was an inner turmoil to just be different. I have spoken extensively about purpose in chapter 6.

But until I went through that depressive state and almost ended my life, I did not find faith for myself.

Faith gives you something to hold on to even when life fires its darts at you.

Faith becomes your shield to ward the darkness off.

After struggling to make sense of life, I finally surrendered my life to Christ so he could lead me.

Just trusting that he has the master-plan in his hands and day-by-day unfolds it to me as I spend time in the presence his just tending and developing a father-daughter relationship with him.

I am passionate about helping the young people find that missing link to a fruitful, joyful, disciplined and massively successful living.

As a pastor and evangelist, I am helping to breed a new generation of influential young people of faith who are helping others find meaning and joy in life. I do this by offering different seminars/workshops in churches, schools, charity organizations and holding online master classes. The topics covered are tailored to the needs of the different organizations after appropriate surveys have been carried out. The topics covered include the following: The power of a positive self-image; Stand up and be counted (Dealing with Bullying); Success-fast track; Speaking for Influence; The confidence code; Winning after a loss etc.

Faith teaches you the principles of affirmation. If you see it, say it, then you can have it.

Great female leaders *are* people of faith.

Chapter 11

FAMILY: THE GLUE THAT HOLDS SUCCESS ALL TOGETHER

True wealth, success and happiness can only be achieved by balancing our business lives with the duty we have towards our self and our family

—Joseph C Kunz, Jr.

While we seek for self-actualization and meaning in life, a woman's success cannot be fully complete without the family. SUPERwomen build strong families.

It takes a woman to build a home and a healthy nation is the one with the healthy family culture. A family is defined as father, mother and the children.

The place of the father cannot be overstated. Although the woman uses a lot of wisdom in getting things going, a girl child would always look up to her father as her first hero.

If the father gets it wrong, the girl-child might likely get it wrong in relationships with the opposite sex except for a few, having developed 'internal relationship compass'.

It's either she goes into relationship with someone like her dad or someone completely opposite.

Olayinka Bello, a gender mainstream expert with the USAID, says 'Although my dad was not much around due to busy work schedules, the precious time spent together were filled with him giving several important lessons of which one is ' never take laws into your own hands.'

This has helped her grow into a calm woman, knowing that nemesis will always catch up with anyone that intentionally offends her. Her mum was a disciplinarian who made her to believe that success comes by diligent hard work and also instilled in her the courage to stand out from the crowd.

The family is the unit of the nation and unity in the family must be promoted by all arms of government to further strengthen the nation.

As a mother of three children myself, I know SUPERwomen have to wear many hats: mom, chef, chauffeur, coach, wife, sister, moderator, negotiator, colleague, boss and many, many more.

There are times I have been torn between going for a business meeting or going out to cheer my son up at a football event. It is a constant feeling.

Having worked with different amazing and successful women spanning the globes as a coach, I have discovered that the struggle to maintain life, career and family is a daily and continuous one.

As women, we're great caretakers and will put the needs and priorities of others first but over time this only leads to failure.

What I've consistently seen is that most women think, 'I just can't have it all.' They're resigned to the thinking that somewhere in their busy days something has to give and most times they're the one left holding the short stick. Often overlooking their own health and well being in order to take care of all the competing priorities of their career and family.

So can you actually 'have your cake and eat it too?'

Yes, you can! It all begins with the mindset! Your health and well being matters.

Get some of these habits and you are on your way to SUPERdom!

Winning Habits to Avoid Getting Burnt-out

1. Get your values right

Your values and purpose are your internal compasses for how to best utilize the natural gifts, talents and genius that you uniquely have to express in the world through your work. When you can walk your path and remain true to your values and gifts, it naturally reduces the amount of stress you experience as you honour yourself and your spirit in all that you think, say, and do in each day.

I choose to set my compass to 'Joyful' in the morning and so I wake everyone up that way. We get out of bed with a smile.

Yes, I am still having a bit of challenge to get my boys to the immediate smiling mode quick enough but my SUPERgirl , Nicole is a shining example to them.

2. Put Your Health First

You need lots of positive energy to be a SUPERwoman! So, take care of your health. I start my day by praying and meditating in the morning, then my workouts.

If your energy level is low, how would you be able to take care of the other important people and things in your life? Your spouse's and children's demeanour are largely influenced by you. It's a massive responsibility but believe me, you have all it takes in you.

Be sure to eat healthy foods that feed your body with good nutrition, and make time for some kind of regular exercise so you can work out the stresses of everyday life. If you don't, these stressors can build up in your system and lead to a variety of health issues both mental and physical, so be proactive in taking good care of yourself. Your loved ones will thank you!

3. Adopt Appropriate Communication

We tend to assume our partners can read our minds. We have lots going through our minds yet if we do not discuss them; we are opening up ourselves to hurt. I do struggle at times with this myself, especially when it comes to sharing my 'lofty' dreams with my husband.

Why? I feel he might think me crazy for always coming up with 'weird' ideas. He is the one that balances me out. He is a phlegmatic and me a sanguine.

So instead of just holding it all in your head and getting all stressed out, practice having open, honest and heartfelt conversations with your loved ones so all involved feel seen, heard and respected. Your spouse and children will appreciate it

4. Get Regularly Refreshed

Statistics has it that up to 50% females working in a corporate environment tend to have their lunches at their desks and this has contributed to workplace 'stress feeling.' If you are part of this statistics, then it's time to make a change.

Be sure to take time out for things that rejuvenate your spirit. Things like meditation, prayer, getting a massage or manicure/pedicure, or taking a walk during your lunch break and singing are all great ways to reduce stress and re-invigorate. Anytime I personally feel stressed, I take a walk and sing. At times at the top of my voice, smiling and waving 'hi' to anyone who looks at me 'incredulously.' Find a few ways that work for you and practice them regularly.

5. Reward Yourself

You have worked really hard, joggling several tasks with work; it's time to think of rewarding yourself.

Just like you would your child after they have done a task or chore successfully, do same for yourself. It uplifts your spirit.

Carrying out a survey of some female entrepreneurs, I discovered that 60% of respondents reward themselves by going shopping. This makes me smile.

Shopping for shoes, handbags, perfumes and even makeup can lighten one's mood and ease tension.

6. The 100% Giving and Receiving rule

It's often said that being in a relationship is a give and take. That you each give 50% to the whole of the relationship to make it 'work' at 100%. But the real key is to give 100% of yourself, your attention and your time in the moment, to your loved ones while asking them to give 100% of themselves to the relationship as well.

In other words, when you're with your significant other (or with a colleague for that matter), be there fully in the moment with them as best you can. When you give your all, they can feel it. And as human beings, when we feel seen and heard fully, our hearts open and it creates a stronger connection with another.

This helps to build trust and collaboration which goes a long way towards reducing misunderstandings.

7. Set Your Priorities

What is the most important thing in your life above all else? What is the second most important thing in your life? The third thing that is most important in your life? When you're clear on what needs to be prioritized first, then it's less stressful to make choices and decisions based on your priorities as you honour your values, heart and spirit.

7. Get the 'Sleep' Therapy

Getting enough sleep is super important! It's the time when your body can process through the stress of the day and rejuvenate your cells. Studies have shown that a lack of sleep can create a multitude of negative effects, such as loss of attention span and productivity, forgetfulness, depression, weight gain, premature aging of your skin, and health risks such as high blood pressure, heart disease and diabetes, just to name a few.

If stress has you worrying and keeping you up at night, try various mindfulness meditations before you go to bed to slow down your system and calm your mind for a restful night's sleep. Your body will thank you and so will everyone else around you.

8. Know Your Boundaries

What are you willing and not willing to do for your work? Where do you draw the line between work time and family time? When does your work-day begin and end? When is your sacred time with family and loved ones? If need be, put it on your calendar and color code it.

The more you practice honouring these boundaries, the more you're honouring your core values. You're also establishing separate neural pathways in your brain for those different areas of your life. As you do this, it becomes easier to 'code switch' or change gears in your mindset to leave work at work and be fully present with friends and family.

9. Rid yourself of 'Energy Drainers'

The people in your inner circle of influence are very important to your outlook to life. If you are surrounded by highly energetic people, you tend to be highly energetic. If surrounded by low energy' people, they tend to drain your energy. It's operates by the law of osmosis.

Energy drainers are those people that are continually negative in their outlook to life or who do not want you to be more successful than them. If you aspire, they tend to feel threatened.

Limit your exposure to them or get out of that circle fast!

10. Release Your Inner Creativity

We all have some kind of creativity that comes through us. Yours could be dancing, singing, gardening, writing, painting, knitting etc.

Mine is singing. I sing when I take walks. It helps release any form of tension in me and focuses my mind on gratitude.

I am presently working on learning to play the keyboard to enhance this part of me. Look out for my musical single or album.

When you take time to express your inner creativity, it allows your right brain to light up and activates various pleasure centers in your brain. This releases a cascade of happy chemicals such as dopamine and serotonin which leaves you feeling good and creates a positive ripple effect into other areas of your life. Life is good, so plan to experience it.

11. Raise up Your Hands for Help

I have always been very independent and loves to have it all done by myself. Why? It feels like I am the only one that can get it done 'perfectly'. This couldn't have been farther from the truth!

Get help! You can train up your children or other family members to help with stuffs around the house.

12. Schedule Regular Play Dates

Just as much as your kids need play dates with their friends, so do you with your significant other and girl friends. Taking time out to let your hair down and be your 'adult' self instead of Mom, or boss, or colleague creates downtime for your hard working brain to just have some fun.

Know those things that only you can do and get help to cover the rest. This way, you get more done and leave yourself some 'me' time. We all want to be of service to others, so remember that you are helping your 'helpers' to feel great by according them the opportunity to help you.

In conclusion, the power to be a world leader is in your hands. The world is in need of women and girls that will step up to the challenge to lead in every facets of life. The human mind is filled with so much potential that we might not fully tap into its fullness. No one can stop you! No one can stop the next generation with you mentoring them. The whole difference you can make starts with a decision.

Have you decided?

I decided long before I was 7 years old to be a leader. To some people, it might sound brazen but to me, it is just who I wanted to be. I was hungry for more and I still am.

The greatness of the mustard tree is in the seed.

Every girl has the tendency to grow into greatness if properly mentored. I was a SUPERgirl who has grown to be a SUPERwoman and I am on a mission to help schools, religious organizations, charities and nations to tap into the full economy of their female resources. My team and I would also be reaching out to the uttermost part of the world, inspiring the next generation through the 'Walk like a princess' charity.

Our mission is to inspire and motivate the female gender to confidently excel in all human endeavours.

To see what we do and donate, visit www.walklikeaprincess.org or www.waliaprin.org

REFERENCES

Maxwell, John C.. *21 Irrefutable Laws of Leadership*. Thomas Nelson, 2007.

Brady, Karen. *Strong Woman: Ambition, Grit and a Great Pair of Heels*. HarperCollins, 2012.

Worre, Eric. *Go Pro*. Network marketing pro, 2013.

Covey, Steven R.. *The 7 habits of Highly Effective People*. Simon & Schuster, 1989

Hansen, Mark Victor. *The Richest Kids in America*. Hansen House, 2009.

INTERNET RESOURCES

http://ctb.ku.edu/en/table-of-contents/structure/strategic-planning/vision-mission-statements/main

http://www.biography.com/people/angela-merkel-9406424#first-female-chancellor

http:// http://www.forbes.com/sites/shelliekarabell/2015/08/03/daughters-and-leadership-influencing-theceo/www.un.org/en/globalissues/ briefingpapers/endviol/

http://ctb.ku.edu/en/table-of-contents/structure/strategic-planning/vision-mission-statements/main

http://www.danijohnson.com/2013/recruiting-irreplaceable-employees/

http://www.forbes.com/sites/kensundheim/2013/04/02/15-traits-of-the-ideal-employee/

http://www.examiner.com/article/mother-teresa-s-lessons-for-our-modern-world-religious-sensitivity

http://firecareers.com/blog/the-building-of-a-vision-statement/

http://www.theguardian.com/society/patrick-butler-cuts-blog/2011/nov/29/ 300k-extra-public-sector-jobs-face-axe

http://www.unwomen.org/en/what-we-do/leadership-and-political-participation/facts-and-figures#sthash.743tBhxR.dpuf

http://www.unwomen.org/en/what-we-do/leadership-and-political-participation/facts-and-figures#sthash.743tBhxR.dpuf

http://www.examiner.com/article/mother-teresa-s-lessons-for-our-modern-world-religious-sensitivity

http://www.elegantwoman.org/good-table-manners.html
http://christinekane.com/how-to-make-a-vision-board/

http://www.theguardian.com/women-in-leadership/2015/jun/11/when-i-started-working-in-technology-i-could-count-the-number-of-women-on-one-hand

http://hubpages.com/hub/Business-dinner-etiquette-where-are-your-manners

ABOUT THE AUTHOR

Sheun is the nation's #1 self- leadership and confidence expert. With over 20 years experience of being a top sales and marketing executive ,trainer and having served as executive and image coach to several clients, she has devoted her life to coaching, training and inspiring the next generation of female leaders.

A frequent speaker at business events, non-profit organizations and on the radio, she has been featured in several newspapers/magazines including The Guardian and has won several awards; she is very passionate about helping individuals, employees and entrepreneurs. She believes that self-leadership is the secret to personal and professional excellence and gender should not stop anyone from attaining life's goals.

She has a first degree in Agricultural economics (Btech) with a focus on gender issues, MBA (marketing management) and later became a certified project & risk manager.

She is the CEO of Loquats consulting LLC –focusing on leadership, communication and mindset training. She is also the founder of Waliaprin (walk-like-a-princess) an organization with the mission to raise the female economy of nations through the use of empowerment programs, seminars and trainings to build the confidence of girls and women.

She is a certified member of the John C Maxwell's legacy team.

Above all, she is a wife, mother of three children and a minister of the gospel with a passion to make music.

To book her to speak at your next corporate event visit www.Sheunoke.com

You can also follow Sheun on these sites:

Twitter: @sheunolotu_oke

Instagram : @seunoke

Periscope: @Sheunolotu_oke

Public page: Sheun Olotu-Oke

Free Tickets to Sheun's Next Live Event in a Location Near You!

To get two free tickets to an upcoming SG2SW event in your city, go to

www.supergirl2superwoman.com today!

ACT NOW—SEATING IS LIMITED!

Use VIP code SG2SW—45XPS when requesting your free tickets.

*For upcoming dates and locations for this international seminar, or to reserve your complimentary seats email sheun@ sheunoke.com or visit www.supergirl2superwoman.com

www.ingramcontent.com/pod-product-compliance
Lightning Source LLC
Chambersburg PA
CBHW061331220326
41599CB00026B/5127